Star Wars Jedi: Survivor: The Complete Official Guide & Walkthrough

DAVID ADAMS

Copyright © 2024 David Adams

All rights reserved.

ISBN-13: 9798878159937

Star Wars Jedi: Survivor: The Complete Official Guide & Walkthrough

CONTENTS

Introduction 1
Game Guide 6
    Tips and Tricks 6
    List of all companions 7
    Difficulty levels 8
    Lightsaber combat stances 9
    Best skills 12
Walkthrough 14
    Main Quests Walkthrough 14
        Find Greez 19
        Find Gyro Module 21
        The Forest Array 23
        Meet Cere on Jedha 26
        Research Tanalor 28
        Reach Pilgrim's Sanctuary 31
        Locate Brother Armias 32
        Bring Contact Codes to Cere 33
        Rescue Zee from the Lucrehulk 34
        Locate Rayvis on the Shattered Moon 36
        Confront Dagan at the Koboh Observatory 37
        Bring Compass to Cordova on Jedha 40
        Locate Bode 41
        Align Arrays at Koboh Control Center 42
Secrets and Collectibles 43
    Unique Collectibles 43
        Stim Canisters 43
        Map Updates 46
        Mysterious Keycode 48

Star Wars Jedi: Survivor: The Complete Official Guide & Walkthrough

Force Tears	49
All fish	56
Coruscant	58
Rooftops	58
Renovation Site 4733	60
Industrial Stacks	61
Undercity Meats	62
Freight Handling Depot	63
Skylane Regulation Station	64
Hangar 2046-C	64
Koboh	65
Gorge Crash Site	65
Winding Ravine	68
Water Treatment Works	70
Corroded Silo	71
Chamber of Fortitude	72
Flooded Bunker	73
Derelict Dam (Part 1)	75
Derelict Dam (Part 2)	79
Derelict Dam (Part 3)	81
Southern Reach (Part 1)	84
Southern Reach (Part 2)	86
Hunter's Quarry	89
Pyloon's Saloon	93
Sodden Grotto	94
Riverbed Watch	96
Foothilll Falls	98
Smuggler's Tunnels	100
Collapsed Passage	102
Chamber of Duality	103

Phon'Qi Caverns (Part 1) 104

Phon'Qi Caverns (Part 2) 107

Mountain Ascent 109

Chamber of Detachment 112

Fogged Expanse 114

Marl Cavern 117

Imperial Post 8L-055 118

Summit Ridge 120

Observatory Understructure 122

Diagnostics Corridor 123

Observation Deck 125

Rift Passage 126

Viscid Bog 127

Chamber of Connection 129

Loading Gantry 131

Lucrehulk Core 134

Forward Control Tower 136

Yurt Barracks 137

Generator Underbelly 140

Boiling Bluff 142

Swindler's Wash 143

Basalt Rift 145

Chamber of Reason 150

Forest Array 151

Rehabilitation Wing 155

Bilemaw Den 156

Nekko Pools 156

Bygone Settlement 157

Magma Rift Passage 161

Moldy Depths 161

Untamed Downs (Part 1)	162
Untamed Downs (Part 2)	165
Chamber of Clarity	167
Fort Kah'Lin	168
Harvest Ridge	171
Alignment Control Center	173
Devastated Settlement (Part 1)	174
Devastated Settlement (Part 2)	178
Rambler's Reach Outpost (Part 1)	180
Rambler's Reach Outpost (Part 2)	183
Jedha	186
Monastery Walls on Jedha	186
Penitent Chambers	189
Halls of Ranvell	190
Divine Oasis	192
Sheltered Hollow	192
Desert Passages	193
Trailhead Pantheon	194
Blustery Mesa	195
Crypt of Uhrma	196
Singing Ruins	197
Sepulcher Pass	198
Veiled Hangar	198
The Archive	199
Path of Persistence	201
Path of Restoration	202
Path of Conviction	203
Wayfinder's Tomb	203
Timeworn Bridge	205
Arid Flats	206

Desert Ridge	209
Narkis Highlands	211
Whistling Drop	212
Sanctuary Temple	213
Buried Refuge	214
Shattered Moon	215
Cargo Loading Deck	215
Automated Forge	215
Assembly Staging	218
Superstructure Fabricators	220
Array Channel	220
Republic Research Laboratory	222
Nova Garon	224
Hanga Bay Exterior	224
Hangar Bay	224
Central Command	225
Officer's quarters	227
Tanalorr	227
Planet Tanalorr	227

Star Wars Jedi: Survivor: The Complete Official Guide & Walkthrough

Introduction

Star Wars Jedi: Survivor builds on the already-winning formula of Star Wars Jedi: Fallen Order by making Cal Kestis a more powerful and resourceful Jedi Knight, while also upping the stakes and the challenges he's facing. Exhilarating lightsaber combat and physics-defying platforming puzzle challenges remain the best part of Respawn's latest Star Wars game, but Survivor also makes big swings with its story this time around. Cal's quest takes him to new corners of the galaxy, but the most compelling journey he makes is an introspective one. Survivor is a very well-written tale about overcoming fear, and it's the Jedi story I've wanted for a long time.

Survivor takes place about five years after the events of Fallen Order, with the Mantis crew having gone their separate ways to pursue different goals in a galaxy increasingly dominated by the Galactic Empire. After a daring escape from Imperial authorities, protagonist Cal finds himself on the planet Koboh, where he discovers a High Republic Jedi protocol droid who carries a clue to reaching Tanalorr, a supposedly unreachable mythical planet. Seeing a potential home that's free of the Empire's influence, Cal sets about reassembling the Mantis crew for another galactic scavenger hunt, but his efforts are waylaid by a former High Republic Jedi who--having originally discovered Tanalorr decades prior and bid his time until the right moment--wants Tanalorr for his own purposes.

The High Republic is a fascinating time period for Survivor to connect its story to given what we know has transpired between that era and the events of post-Revenge of the Sith. The comics describe The High Republic as the golden age of the Jedi. And that may be the case, but we also know this time period will culminate in the Jedi Order led by Master Yoda, who preached to a young Anakin Skywalker that "fear is the path to the Dark Side." Not anger. Not grief. Not any of the other emotions a Jedi is supposed to unhealthily suppress. The events of the High Republic teach the Jedi that fear is the path to evil--the other emotions are just stepping stones along it.

Survivor runs with that idea, exploring the concept of fear and what it means for someone like Cal, a survivor of both a war and a genocidal attack on his people, to live with the ever-present shadow of fear. As a survivor of the Jedi Order, Cal fears failing to live up to its ideals, compelling him to go to unhealthy extremes in his fight against the Empire. All the while, he pushes down the growing sentiment he feels for those he loves in order to avoid painful rejection.

While the theme of fear and how it can change you is central to Cal's journey, Survivor's main antagonists also benefit from this focus, transforming into foils for Cal to reflect on his actions. On their own, the two big bads lack the level of nuanced characterization I want from a villain--in the end, both boil down to being evil because they're selfish, albeit in different ways. It's not exactly compelling when compared to Fallen Order's terrifying and yet understandably tragic Second Sister. But as foils for Cal, Survivor's villains catalyze his growth. First, forcing him to come to terms with how his reckless pursuit of destroying the Empire and reaching Tanalorr could culminate in his own fall to the Dark Side if he's not careful. And second, recognizing the importance of being a new type of Jedi for a changed galaxy.

We've seen variations of these transformations in Jedi before--Luke Skywalker and Ahsoka Tano being the two major examples in the current canon. But in Cal's journey, Respawn delves even deeper into what it means for a Jedi grappling with the doubts and insecurities that everyday people in the Star Wars universe navigate all the time. Cal did not grow up as a normal kid like Luke nor did he have a non-traditional mentor as a padawan like Ahsoka. As a result, his attempts to wrestle with his fears of obsession and commitment are more tenuous and susceptible to outside influence than the Jedi we've seen safely balance their internal light and darkness before.

As a result, Cal's conflict with Survivor's villains sees him regularly teetering toward the Dark Side more than the typical Star Wars protagonist (save for Anakin Skywalker, obviously), leaving you guessing up until the final fight of the game as to where Cal's moral compass is eventually going to align. That seesaw ride is so poignant because Survivor's story gives Cal a lot to care about and isn't afraid to see him lose it during crucial narrative beats. The narrative incentive of Survivor isn't a desire to see the good guys win, it's to explore just how much the good guys are willing to throw away on their path to victory.

While these new personal challenges require a great deal of growth from Cal to grapple with, the more immediate physical challenges rely on a familiar set of skills and abilities. Survivor smartly avoids the pitfall of depowering its protagonist, meaning Cal starts off with the lightsaber and traversal abilities he earned during Fallen Order. Against the weaker foes of the early game, Cal already feels suitably dominant, as a seasoned Jedi that has been fighting for survival should be. You are empowered to slice through simple Storm Troopers and perform Force-propelled parkour across bottomless pits with ease. These skills don't mean Cal is all-powerful, though, and after an exciting opening chapter, Survivor puts you in your place with an assortment of challenging new enemy types. This encourages you to spend your points wisely in Survivor's branching skill tree to unlock new powers.

Similar as Fallen Request, Survivor's battle essentially depends on Cal's lightsaber, cutting through a foe's watchman and repelling their strikes until their endurance gives out so you can land a few strong hits. It's a lot simpler to observe approaching assaults from fakeouts or preplanned wind-ups in Survivor contrasted with Fallen Request, and Cal's moves feel more keen and speedier this time around, as well. This manages the cost of you more control during the most intense part of the conflict and assists the game's for the most part speedy battles with feeling more conquerable. At the point when a foe gets a hit in, it presently feels more like your misstep and not an unfortunate turn of events where the shine of Cal's lightsaber and molecule impacts of a foe's weapon ruined the visual language of the repel specialist.

Cal has his own endurance meter to stress over, so battle is as much about control and cautious timing for what it's worth about being decisively forceful. Each fight works out as a cerebral activity; the experience develops with a thrilling stream as you get its hang, which is all caught with extraordinary sound detail. Each painstakingly diverted blaster bolt resonates with that unmistakable Star Wars ping; the murmur of Cal's lightsaber and the compacted transition of Power energy assist with selling the invigorating rush of playing as a Jedi Knight.

However BD-1 is as yet your standard buddy who keeps you recuperated up and opens entryways, Cal is joined by different characters during specific pieces of the story as well. Either the blaster-hauling Bode or magick-using Merrin joins Cal in specific story missions to assist him with managing harder battles. Neither one of the ones adds anything particularly vital to the experience of battle yet they are a welcome asset for swarm control in the hard core battles in the last 50% of the game, and their tag-group takedowns with Cal are visual enjoyments.

To oblige the possibility that he's currently more seasoned and more talented, Cal likewise gets two new lightsaber positions in Survivor: Blaster and Crossguard. The previous offers Cal a went battling style while the last option bargains in sluggish yet weighty strikes. Both enjoy their benefits, however Blaster feels improved moving, matching the other three styles in feeling of speed. Cal feels most grounded while he's winding through a horde of foes, diverting blaster bolts and rapidly striking his rival at the times their gatekeeper flounders, and that is only trickier to do with the more slow Crossguard style.

Survivor restricts you to just having two lightsaber positions prepared at an at once, to visit a reflection circle designated spot to transform them. Now and again, this limitation can feel disappointing as it pipes how you spend your expertise focuses into the two styles you at last wind up utilizing most frequently, subsequently putting trial and error down. Also, since you just get one free expertise respec per playthrough there's little an open door to investigate what could be fascinating new capacities and approaches. You can respec in the wake of utilizing the gift, however you need to surrender one of your expertise focuses each time.

While I at first viewed this as smothering, I came to see the value in how the restriction constrained me to adjust to where I allotted my ability focuses, particularly when it came to lightsaber positions. Each style has its own interesting assets and shortcomings, so you can arrange your own interpretation of how Cal battles. You choose where Cal misses the mark - swarm control, for instance, or perhaps full scale assault power- - and afterward get imaginative by they way you conquer that shortcoming. I selected to zero in on the handyman Single position and reach centered Blaster position, for example, which made Cal a monster at dueling one-on-one. Notwithstanding, I endured during battle experiences where the game tossed twelve foes all at once at me. In those cases, I rested on Power capacities to assist Cal with slowing down specific enemies long enough so I wouldn't be overpowered. It seemed like I had the option to make my own one of a kind rendition of Cal who spent significant time in this tomfoolery quick in and out battling style that at last brought me through to the credits.

Platforming difficulties and Power puzzles return in Survivor too. Like battle, both feel improved in Survivor in contrast with Fallen Request - Cal naturally hooks onto climbable surfaces now, and a solid grouping of unlockable easy routes implies that unintentionally missing a leap halfway through an activity set piece probably won't slow down you excessively far. Survivor has a supportive clue framework, as well. All the more critically, it regards your knowledge, possibly springing up in the event that you leave the game sitting while you're amidst a riddle or you appear to be stuck. And, surprisingly, then, at that point, as Fallen Request, the game will inquire as to whether you'd like a clue first rather than simply providing you some insight by and large - that is a welcome degree of limitation. It simply

Star Wars Jedi: Survivor: The Complete Official Guide & Walkthrough

proposed to give me indicates two times, the twice during puzzles I super couldn't sort out where to go or what to do. I don't have the foggiest idea how Survivor realized which puzzles I needed to get some margin to sort out and which I frantically required a hint for, yet it did.

Survivor is at its best when each component - story, battle, and puzzle platforming- - impacts along with excited energy in a manner that is quintessentially Star Wars. This is generally clear in one of the game's most critical features, a manager quarrel over halfway through the game. The second highlights portions of battle, platforming, and a significant story result, in which Cal and Merrin cooperate to obliterate a Supreme mining device, joining Jedi capacities and Nightsister magick in a strained, true to life experience where your responses are scrutinized and Survivor's outright banger of a soundtrack is enlarging in your ears. Everything comes full circle in the two partners bringing down the machine with one of the coolest completing moves I've found in any Star Wars project. I really stood up from my sofa and cheered when it worked out - you can see that the group behind this game sees exactly the way in which cool Star Wars can be.

The game sets aside a few minutes for calm minutes as well, best found in one more of Survivor's major new elements: a center point like region that Cal can get back to regularly. On Koboh, Cal can visit a bar that loads up with NPCs you've saved money on your movements across the world. A portion of these characters go about as merchants, selling Cal beauty care products or discretionary interactivity advantages. Others assist Cal with brightening up the bar with music or a roof garden. The best of them go about as journey providers, pointing Cal towards the riddle boxes that are High Republic vaults, abundance tracker small managers, or more recruitable NPCs. Regardless of whether the actual characters are, generally, narratively level and exhausting to converse with, the advantages they sell are fulfilling and the missions they give you are much of the time amusing to finish. Caij Vanda is my number one - she assists you with finding the Haxion Brood abundance trackers who are coming for Cal after he got away from their grip in Fallen Request. These abundance trackers are regularly deft warriors with jetpacks, blasters, deployable safeguards, and a wide exhibit of contraptions obviously appropriate for overpowering a Power client. Finding them makes for a few fabulously tense duels, and the prizes Caij gives Cal for doing probably the most incredible in the game are as well.

On a last note, Survivor's specialized presentation is a hindrance that should be noted. Playing on Xbox Series X, I encountered irregular accidents on various events, all annoyingly during cutscenes before the game got an opportunity to autosave. On one unfortunate (and profoundly baffling) event, the game crashed during the cutscene following a particularly difficult different stage supervisor battle that had taken me many endeavors to beat at last. As a result of the accident, my advancement was lost and I needed to battle the manager multiple times once more, procuring a triumph that felt a lot more empty than whenever I first beat him. On PlayStation 5, a partner revealed some periodic faltering, screen-tearing, and crashing as well, and the PC form likewise has different specialized issues connecting with in-game show, execution, and equipment enhancement.

Survivor expands on Fallen Request in more than one way, straightening out the battle mechanics, growing the assortment of lightsaber styles, reducing the disappointment of platforming and riddles, and diving into less-standard Star Wars legend to recount a Jedi attempting to overcome a domineering evil no matter what and arriving at the place of understanding that you can't simply battle for good- - you need to battle for good in the correct manner. It's a great Star Wars game that gets into the bare essential of the battle of the stuff for a Jedi Knight to start the excursion toward the position of Expert.

Game Guide

Tips and Tricks

Learn to parry

Parrying enemy attacks is the best way to quickly take the initiative. It is worth giving your opponent time to attack so that you can parry it and quickly break through their defenses. If you succeed, the enemy will be vulnerable for a short while.

Avoid red attacks

Some attacks cannot be blocked and parried. They are easy to spot, as the opponent then begins to glow red. This means that the attack is powerful enough to break through your defense. In such situations, you must dodge. If you evade this attack, the opponent will have to recover from the missed attack for a short while.

Scan new enemies and objects

By doing a quick scan, not only will you learn new things about a particular object or enemy, but, on top of that, you will receive a small amount of experience points.

Return to the place of your last death

Each death will reset your previous experience bar to zero. To regain the lost experience, you must go to the place where you died last time or defeat the enemy who killed you. What's more, this will also restore some of your health. The death marker is visible on the map, so you will always know which way to go.

Explore all locations

This way you will rapidly secure different parts like materials, restorative things and even advantages. By visiting such places you can likewise get a lot of involvement focuses, or find unique places where you can build your most extreme wellbeing or Power level.

Use the hints

A few riddles can be difficult to settle. In the event that you can't tackle them, in some cases it merits utilizing a clue. By conversing with BD-1, Cal frequently thinks of a thought worth paying attention to. This way you will know immediately how you really want to advance the riddle.

List of all companions

Jedi Survivor has the option to use the support of companions controlled by artificial intelligence. On this page of the guide you will find **a list of Cal's available companions** who can travel with him under certain circumstances. We also write about skills of your allies and when you can meet the next companions.

BD-1

The friendly droid has appeared in Jedi Fallen Order. It continues to travel with Cal almost throughout the entire game. BD-1 will join the main character shortly after the start of the new campaign and will remain with him.

BD-1 can primarily heal the main character with stims - you can gradually increase their supply during the game.

The droid is also able to manipulate objects from the environment. BD-1 can, for example, hack devices or open passageways.

Bode Akuna

Bode Akuna is an explorer who is one of Cal's new companions. He shows up while you visit Coruscant toward the start of the game. He will then turn into an impermanent friend and travel along with Cal for some time.

Bode can assist you in battles and you with canning additionally request him which rivals to assault. The gunman likewise has a stream pack and can control objects from the climate and, for instance, move something or open a spot for the hero to climb.

You can peruse more about this friend at Who is Bode Akuna?. Cautioning - this page might contain spoilers!

Night Sister Merrin

Merrin is a Night Sister well known from Jedi Fallen Order. In the new campaign, you will meet her while exploring the planet Jedha. She will then become a temporary companion and travel together with Cal for a while.

Merrin can fight and she has a very useful ability to temporarily stop opponents. The Night Sister can teleport and help Cal climb by unlocking new places for the climbing rope.

Difficulty levels

Story mode

As the name recommends, this is a mode for individuals who need to zero in mostly on the game's story rather than the battle and the test. The edge for mistake here is extremely high, you have a lot of opportunity to perform pairings, and what's more, the rivals are not exceptionally forceful and bargain less harm.

Jedi Padawan

This is a mode similar to the easy difficulty level. The aggression of enemies and the damage they inflict is slightly higher relative to the story mode. However, it still will be hard to die fighting them. This level is for the players who do not want the combat to be too demanding.

Jedi Knight

This is the ordinary trouble level. In the event that you are know all about the class and are searching for a reasonable test as far as battle, then, at that point, this mode is ideally suited for you. Adversaries are significantly more liable to make a hostile move and incur impressive harm, though still inside the limits of presence of mind. An opportunity to appropriately repel a foe assault is more limited - in any case, after a couple of effective endeavors, you will rapidly start, and diverting hits will turn out to be simple.

Jedi Master

The Jedi Expert compares to the hard troublesome level, and it's focused on individuals who need to make the game essentially more challenging for themselves. An opportunity to repel an assault is more limited, rivals are bound to go after you, and the customary foe can turn into a significant danger. We most certainly don't suggest this mode for individuals who need to zero in on going after without contemplating protection or strategies.

Jedi Grand Master

This is the most difficult of all available difficulty levels. It is aimed at experienced players and those who have completed the game at least once. This mode will be an excellent choice if you care about dynamics and challenges. However, keep in mind that even a tegular droid will be able to kill you with one accurate attack.

Additional facilities

As well as picking the trouble level, players can likewise involve a few in-game offices. They can be found in the game's settings, all the more explicitly in the ongoing interaction tab. In the "Battle" segment, impairing the Fast Time Events is conceivable.

In the mean time, in the "Investigation" segment, there is a choice liable for fall harm. You can likewise switch it off. If, then again, the fight is occurring at a speed that is excessively quick for you, you can go lower in the settings to empower the Sluggish Mode. This will make it a lot more straightforward for you to respond to the activities of the foes.

Lightsaber combat stances

Best stance

Cal at any given time can have 2 stances at the ready and use one of them. Our recommendations are:

- Dual Wield- This stance will allow you to make a series of quick attacks. Its added advantage is easier automatic pairing thanks to the focused pairing skill (this does not include red attacks).

- Crossguard - This is the ideal posture for mounting very powerful attacks. They are slow, so this will only work on selected types of enemies and in situations where the enemy has been stunned.

We discuss all 5 attitudes in more detail below.

Stance #1 - Single

Cal uses a single-handed lightsaber. The stance is available from the very beginning of the game and does not need to be unlocked.

Single is the most balanced stance, which has no clear strengths or weaknesses.

Stance #2 - Double-bladed

Cal utilizes a lightsaber with 2 edges. You will open this position soon after the start of the game. Cal will show up on Coruscant to a gathering of stormtroopers and an instructional exercise on exchanging between various positions will be started.

It's a decent position for going after gatherings of foes and for redirecting steady fire by adversaries furnished with blasters. Its hindrances are lower strength and more terrible reach.

Stance #3 - Dual wield

Cal holds a different lightsaber in each hand. You will open this stanceduring the conflict with the 10th Sister chief. This is the subsequent significant supervisor to be crushed on Coruscant.

It's a position for making speedy assaults, yet the reach is seriously decreased. It's additionally worth utilizing the extremely helpful centered matching (hold down Triangle/Y), which is able to do naturally avoiding foes' ordinary assaults.

Stance #4 - Crossguard

Cal utilizes a two-gave lightsaber. You will open this position as the final remaining one. It is the award for overcoming the Drya Thornne chief, which you should look on the Annihilated Moon. This is a remarkable area from the universe map visited in the quest for Tanalorr.

This position is made for extremely sluggish yet strong assaults, which can be also charged to cause considerably more harm. It just functions admirably against slow rivals or the people who have been briefly dazed.

Stance #5 - Blaster

Cal all the while utilizes a blaster and a lightsaber. You will open the stanceduring your most memorable visit to the Cere base situated in Jedah. Returning to Mantis, the legend will be come by Bode who will give you a blaster.

It's an excellent position for expanding the viability of run battle. Cal can shoot normal or stacked blaster shots with limitless ammo recovered by going after foes with a lightsaber.

Changing stances

At any given time, Cal can have 2 of the 5 available stances at the ready. Reach any meditation point or any workshop and go to the stances menu. You can set 2 different ones among the ones you have.

Stances can be changed by:

- pressing the left and right directions on the crossbar while playing on the pad;
- pressing X and C while playing on the keyboard.

Improving stances

Every position has its own different ability tree and you can purchase more by burning through at least 1 expertise focuses on them.

With things from the improvement trees, you can open new moves for a given position (for example another way for the block to work), as well as improve and alter definitely known assaults. You ought to update the 2 positions you utilize most frequently in the game first, since expertise focuses amass somewhat leisurely.

Best skills

Resilience tree

Every one of the abilities in this tree are valuable - you ought to get them all in the end. We have incorporated the main ones underneath.

Basic instincts - There are a sum of 3 abilities to open. Every expertise builds Cal's most extreme wellbeing. This will assist Cal with enduring more harm.

Further developed Stim Equation - There are a sum of 2 abilities to open. They assist you with recovering more wellbeing with stims.

Collaboration - This expertise speeds up the mending system with stims. This will lessen the gamble that an adversary assault will intrude on the mending.

Centered Sight - With this expertise you can naturally keep away from scuffle assaults. This expertise is exceptionally useful and connected with one of the prizes. Nonetheless, red assaults can't be stayed away from with it.

Lightsaber trees

On account of abilities connected to positions, their choice ought to rely upon the one you use - you can utilize 2 out of the 5 accessible at some random time. We have depicted the best positions on a different page of the aide.

We encourage you to buy the primary abilities from the expertise trees for somewhere around 2 of your number one positions. Every first expertise in the tree requires just 1 expertise point, and they can add new valuable kinds of assaults for a given position.

Accuracy Delivery from the Double Use tree - This is an expertise connected to one of the prizes. Exceptionally helpful in light of the fact that it expands the adequacy of Centered Repel. You can deliver the repelling button when the rival assaults and make a more grounded counterattack.

Blaster Cooldown from the Blaster tree - This ability permits you to get additional ammo from adversaries by hitting them with your lightsaber. This will permit you to shoot the blaster on a more regular basis.

Dividing Swipe from the Crossguard tree - The Crossguard position is great for slow, strong assaults, as is this ability. You can make a wide swing with the lightsaber, which will cause monstrous harm.

Force trees

There are 3 trees with various aloof and dynamic abilities connected with the Power. Not every one of them are quickly accessible, as, for instance, you will just open the Lift and Hammer Power abilities by progressing in the primary storyline.

Attunement from the Jedi Fixation tree - There are a sum of 3 abilities to open. Every expertise builds Cal's greatest Power. This will permit you to utilize every one of the assaults and moves that utilization the Power on a more regular basis.

More noteworthy Hold from the Jedi Fixation tree - This expertise expands the impact of Slow Mode. You will actually want to bargain more goes after to adversaries impacted with the Sluggish Mode.

Diverted Energy from the Jedi Fixation tree - This expertise further develops the Power recuperation while going after foes (you will get the most focuses for killing them).

Taking off Lift and Mass Ram from the Supernatural power tree - These are better variants of Lift and Hammer Power abilities. You can utilize these capacities on gatherings of rivals and not simply individual targets.

Befuddled Psyche from the Confound tree - There are a sum of 2 abilities to open, which can delay the impact of brain control. This is particularly helpful in the event that you have utilized Confound on major areas of strength for a.

More prominent Disarray from the Befuddle tree - This expertise permits you to utilize mind control on 2 rivals.

Tips on buying skills

- Skills require spending 1 or more skill points to unlock them. Don't ignore the more expensive ones, because chances are good that they offer great profits.

- You can check how a skill works before buying it. The game has short videos, showing, for example, how a given skill works in combat. This will help you determine whether that particular skill is useful for you.

- You can reset skill trees, and thus get back the skill points you have spent. We discussed this topic in more detail on the page Can you reset skills?

- Pay attention to the "Uses Force" information in skill descriptions. This means that an ability can only be activated if Cal has enough Force in reserve. If not, you will need to wait until it gets restored. Keep this in mind during battles.

Walkthrough
Main Quests Walkthrough

Coruscant

On this page of the Star Wars Jedi Survivor guide, you will find a walkthrough for the story mission on the planet Coruscant. This mission is divided into two main stages, in which you have to get to Senator Daho Sejan's yacht and then escape from the Undercity Meats to the Mantis.

Follow CSF Captain

When the game starts, you will see that Cal Kestis has been brought as a detainee to the planet Coruscant. Follow the escort.

In the end, you will be directed to Representative Sejan, and after a brief time you will realize what is Cal's genuine reason to visit this planet. At the point when you assume command over the person after an easy route scene, you will go through a short battle instructional exercise, during which you should overcome a few rivals - adhere to the on-screen directions.

Pursue the Senator's Yacht

After the fight is finished, watch one more cut-scene. Move along the metal part of the left, take hold of the mesh, go up and afterward to one side.

Hop up and take hold of a metal shaft, then move to one side - you don't need to fear blaster shots discharged by monitors.

Sooner or later, the metal construction will implode - you will fall into the room underneath. Use Power Push to open an entry in the broke wall displayed in the picture above.

Turn left, move to the rooftop, then bounce up to take hold of the bars on the right and afterward move higher.

Climb the line and follow the headings on the screen (drop down to go under the deterrent). You will arrive at a reflection point.

The way proceeds with the slow down displayed in the picture above. There are three adversaries sitting tight for you at the top.

Rout the rivals, then, at that point, transform into the hall behind them. Stroll ahead, use Power Pull to make a section and keep following the way.

Turn left, stroll along the line and get the bars. By bouncing down to the stage underneath, you can promptly kill one of the adversaries. Further way leads through the hole under the neon sign.

You will open a new lightsaber position that you can use to overcome a few rivals.

Snatch the pole and hop forward. When the stormtrooper remaining on the housetop starts terminating at you, hold down the block button not long before you get hit and afterward continue to hold it to redirect all bolts toward the foe.

Use Power Pull, get around the bars and proceed to one side. Watch a cut-scene.

Go with Bode and enact an easy route on the way. You will arrive at a contemplation point where you can rest.

Reunite With Your Crew at the Yacht

Take a gander at the hanging chest and ask Bode to obliterate the snag. Then, at that point, initiate the station to shoot a zipline and use it to get to the following piece of the area.

Follow Bode by making a wall run. At the point when you arrive at the slope, run up the wall on the right and bounce up to join your friend.

Have Bode cut the zipline at the top and afterward climb it to the upper floor. Follow Bode.

Slide down the rooftop, get around the slope and rout adversaries. After the fight, initiate the terminal and get ready for another battle, this time with 3 foes.

At the point when you arrive at an impasse, have Bode move a bulletin for you - climb it. You will arrive at another contemplation point.

Go up the steps and keep following Bode, then, at that point, go to the entryway on the left. There are a few foes inside.

Utilize the bars to leap to another structure, then keep strolling along the line on the right. At the point when you drop down, you should overcome a few rivals and gain proficiency with a superskill.

Continuing on, you will run over another adversary unit. Have Bode bring down the orange-yellow component, then push the close by metal block, and climb it to hop higher.

Bounce up and take hold of the bars to get to the following rooftop, then stumble into the bended announcement - hop close to its finish to take hold of the bars. Run on the following board, get a bar and leap to the following piece of the area.

Cut the rope, then, at that point, use Power Pull on it to leap to the opposite side, getting the bars. Move up. Pushing ahead, open another alternate way.

You will experience a few rivals. Open the orange way to actuate another alternate way. In the event that you need to, utilize the close by reflection point and get ready for a supervisor battle.

Go down the steps. In the spot displayed in the picture above, you will find a hole through which you will arrive at the manager battle field.

In the event that you want assistance overcoming K-405, the main supervisor of Star Wars Jedi Survivor, look at a different page of this aide: How to overcome the K-405 chief?.

After the manager battle, cooperate with the heap of junk toward the edge of the field - you will get the Climb Link.

Utilize the new device to leap to a higher floor. Then utilize the terminal and, hopping starting with one stage then onto the next, head towards the primary mission marker.

Board the Senator's Yacht

After the cut-scene, trust that the partners will bring down the scaffold and open the section. Utilizing the Rising Link, take hold of the grades, and afterward climb upwards, by taking hold of the intuitive components.

At the point when you arrive at the spot displayed in the picture above, hop down.

Use Power Push on the line to move the obstruction and trust that the group will bring down the boat a little.

Snatch the bars under the yacht to continue on. Hop down, utilize the zipline and leap to a higher stage, then use Power Push to eliminate the subsequent hindrance.

Take hold of the bars, then move to one side to board the yacht. Make the way for the vehicle and get to the Representative's terminal.

It doesn't make any difference which exchange choice you pick while conversing with the Congressperson - you'll simply hear a somewhat unique line of discourse.

Escape Undercity Meats

Turn and run the other way - utilize the Climb Link on the get point and bounce further.

Turn left and, utilizing the Climb Link, leap to the upper floor of this area. Continuing on, obliterate the test and do a wall leap to move to a reflection point.

Keep strolling toward the path displayed in the picture above. Utilize the Rising Link to bounce higher. In the wake of overcoming the two tests, pass through the entryway on the left - in the following room, you should battle a more grounded rival.

Open the entryway, go through the dim room and just barely get through the thin hole on the option to get further into the area. You will gain proficiency with the Befuddle expertise.

Continuing on, take hold of one of the moving compartments to leap to the following field - this time you will confront a greater gathering of rivals.

Pass through the entryway, utilize the Rising Link on the get point, then hop towards the wall and skip off it to leap to the more significant level of the area. You will arrive at a contemplation point - rest in the event that you need to, in light of the fact that you are going to battle another chief.

Going on from the reflection point, you will arrive at an extension with a huge number. After a short cut-scene, you will battle the 10th Sister, the second supervisor of Star Wars Jedi Survivor.

Get to the hangar

Request that BD-1 smother the flares and open a section to the following piece of the area. You will arrive at the following contemplation point.

Go down the steps, then, at that point, utilize the lift to plunge to the lower floor. Continuing on, you will arrive at the Skylane Guideline Station, where you should confront three adversaries.

Utilizing the assistance of BD-1, initiate the zipline. You need to go through a fascinating arcade grouping, which comprises of a triple wall run (you need to get to the third bulletin by utilizing the zipline), and toward the end you need to bounce and utilize the zipline to get to the stage.

A little further on you should confront a few rivals. Move up the zipline, then, clutching the mesh, push ahead and leap out so you can utilize the zipline to take hold of the rope displayed in the picture above.

Dropping the rope, you need to hop at the right second over to the rope on the option to proceed with your excursion.

As you enter the overhang, watch a cut-scene with Bado and Brove. Continuing on, you will arrive at a reflection point, and rout more foes while heading to the Mantis.

Clean Up the Mantis

Star Wars Jedi: Survivor: The Complete Official Guide & Walkthrough

Head to the ship's bar and collect an extra outfit for BD-1. Then use the workbench, where you can change the appearance of BD-1 and the lightsaber, as well as your combat stance. Now you can use the ship to fly to the planet Koboh.

Find Greez

This page of the guide to Star Wars Jedi Survivor describes the story mission on the planet Koboh - Find Greez. During this mission, you will have to solve several environmental puzzles, as well as face a boss battle.

Find Greez

Subsequent to leaving Mantis, make a beeline for the left. You should run along the wall and afterward get through the hole.

Presently you will go through an instructional exercise on utilizing the BD Visor - adhere to the directions on the screen to check an animal noticeable somewhere far off. Go on down the slant and bring the lift down to the contemplation point.

Run along the wall and afterward hop between stages to get to the cavern. There you will run over a few B-1 fight droids, joined by another strong rival - the Pandemonium Plunderer. Stroll through the dull cavern until you come to a break in the wall, which you will use to get outside.

Go to the right, hop on the plants, and afterward move to the left. On the precipice you will see a B-1 droid, you can kill it while dangling from a stone rack.

Going ahead, remember to actuate the easy route that prompts the contemplation point. On the wall with a plant, you will find a projection, which you can leap to with a catching snare. Climb the support point to one side, then leap to the following wall and move up.

Run over the wall, and keeping in mind that arrival, attempt to go after the Uproar Plunderer. In the wake of wiping out the B2 droid (you can capture the rockets with the Power and send them back towards them), run along the wall to arrive on a higher stage.

At the point when you arrive at the lake with slime, stroll along the line (it will break sooner or later), and afterward stroll as fast as conceivable to the metal piece. Snatch one of the bombs with the Power, then push the charge toward the dam to raise the stage you are remaining on.

Proceeding, remember to enact another alternate route. At the point when you arrive at another area, proceed with the way. In the wake of arriving at the spot displayed in the picture above, trust that the watch will draw a little nearer and dispose of one foe with a leap assault. Continue to stroll towards the contemplation point.

At the point when you arrive at the fork, take the street on the left, which will take you to the muck tank. Leap to the yellow stage, then, at that point, hop towards the plants and utilize the catching snare to pull yourself to the wall. Move to the highest point of the dam and rout two adversaries.

Proceed with the way to one side. Rout the rivals and enter the cavern on the left.

In the center, you will confront a BX droid. Run up the wall and go on through the cavern and hop down toward the finish of the passage. When you continue on, you should be ready for a battle, since you will be gone after off guard the Clamor Pillager.

At the point when you start the machine on the right, bombs will start emerging from under the ground - be ready to push one of the explosives towards the shining wall to open the section prompting the dam.

Move toward where the bombs show up and , maintaining the right separation, lead the bomb nearer to the muck tank. Then, at that point, snatch it and toss at the component displayed in the screen capture above to make an extension.

Rehash the above move, however this time lead the charge nearer to the dam, then, at that point, push it toward the wall to cause a blast and raise the slop level in the tank.

Bounce between stages (you can step on the sludge for a specific measure of time) to get to the plant, after which you will move up the bluff to the recently stamped area and trigger the cutscene.

From that point forward, bring the lift down, dispose of the droid (it merits utilizing the bomb on the right), and afterward follow the way to the left.

You will arrive at a room with additional foes - there are likewise bombs here that can be utilized in fight. At the point when the battle is finished, move the metal part of the spot displayed in the screen capture above and run up the wall to the more elevated level.

At the point when you're at the top, cut the rope and afterward use it to leap to where the Bogling is sitting tight for you. To get to the reflection point, you should enter a tight upward passage and hop from one wall to another until you arrive at the extremely top. You will arrive at a reflection point.

Continue to stroll along the way leads, and you will ultimately arrive at the town - Drifter's Arrive at Station, where you will find another reflection point. At the point when you arrive at the Pyloon's Cantina, you will initiate a cutscene, after which you will confront a supervisor battle.

The third storyline manager of the Star Wars Jedi Survivor game is Zeik, who is one of the Chaos Looters. This rival is more grounded than different foes of this kind, yet shouldn't lead to many issues. Block Zeik's customary assaults and stay away from red assaults, and you ought to rapidly overcome this chief.

We depicted the battle against Zeik on a different page of this aide: How to overcome the chief - Zeik?.

After the fight is finished, enter the cantina to set off a more extended cutscene, during which Cal will meet his companion Greez.

Rest in the basement

After the cutscene, go down to the basement, where Greez has prepared a room for Cal, where you will find, among other things, a meditation point. Rest on the bed to complete this story task and get a new mission.

Find Gyro Module

On this page of the guide to Star Wars Jedi Survivor you can find a walkthrough for Find Gyro Module - one of the story missions from Koboh. Our guide shows how and where to get the part needed for Mantis repairs, and how to solve the puzzles in Chamber of Duality.

Find Gyro Module

Greez will open an entryway in Cal's room prompting the Dealer's Passages. When you arrive at the pathway impeded by a green power field, turn right and go through an opening in the wall.

Proceed with the way displayed in the screen capture above. Do two wall runs and afterward hop between stages to arrive at the further piece of this area.

Use Power on the wall that block the way forward. Presently you want to arrive at the region with the red sheet - circumvent the room and utilize the bar to get to the right stage.

Interface with the Gyro module to enact a cut-scene.

Bring Gyro Module to Greez

You'll end up at a contemplation point. Bounce onto the blue stage, then, at that point, do a wall run and arrive at the following stage. Leap to the edge underneath and afterward wall run twice to arrive at the following one.

There is a little troublesome segment before you - you really want to do 2 wall runs and afterward hop into a limited passage that leads up (bob off walls). Continue forward and just barely get through an opening in the wall.

You've entered another zone - Office of Duality. Take the circle from the wall on the lt and place it in the system close by to make a scaffold prompting the opposite side.

After the cut-scene, pivot to see the circle which you've utilized minutes prior and Pull it once more. Put it in the system on the left.

Cross the extension. Use Power Push to get a component required for opening the entryway and spot it at the closest anchor.

There is one more circle behind the entryway - Power Pull it, get back with it to the primary stage, and spot it in one of the components.

Presently Pull the circle that you've utilized before and place it in the leftover component.

Cross the recently made span then, at that point, do a wall run on the passed on wall to arrive at the stage. At the point when you arrive at the finish of the stage, hop into the space between two thin walls and go up.

Star Wars Jedi: Survivor: The Complete Official Guide & Walkthrough

Force Pull the component required for the entryway and put it on the anchor on the left. Hop down to the focal stage.

Converse with Zee to initiate an easy route scene. Communicate with the gleaming item to open new an Advantage.

Follow Zee to the lift to get back to Drifter's Arrive at Station. Enter the bar and converse with Greez to complete the job.

The Forest Array

On this page of the guide to Star Wars Jedi Survivor, you will find a walkthrough for the story mission on the planet Koboh - The Forest Array. You will learn how to open the forest gate, how to reach the forest array, and how to go through it return to the Mantis.

Open Forest Gate

Leave the family room and make a beeline for the white-blue entryway noticeable somewhere far off. The way leads through the bluffs on the left, simply do a couple of wall runs and afterward manage a few rivals. You will arrive at a reflection point.

Keep strolling on the left side until you arrive where you notice a Bilemaw.

After the battle, go under the cascade and do a wall rush to arrive at the stone rack. Follow the way.

You will ultimately wind up by a contemplation point on the other side of the imploded span. Dispose of a couple of rivals and leap to climg higher. The door is monitored by two Clamor Thieves. Rout the rivals and before you go further, initiate the alternate way prompting the reflection point. Open the door and enter the forest.

Reach the Forest Array

Follow the way and slice through thick plants hindering the way. At the point when you arrive at an impasse, pivot and run along the wall to the other side of the fracture. Utilizing your lightsaber, slice through the stone support point supporting the stone to frame a scaffold.

Use Power Push on the obstruction displayed in the picture above, then request BD-1 to actuate the zipline and use it to get to the other side. To continue on, you should make a couple of wall rushes to stay away from the tricky stream. Ultimately you will arrive at a contemplation point.

Utilizing the Power, you should take out rock arrangements from the wall and hop between them. In the wake of taking out the third component, you want to hop on the wall and run along it to the plants. This way you will get to the highest point of the bluff.

The way to the super goal leads straight through the door displayed in the picture above. At the point when you get to the other side of the crack, proceed with the way on the right.

You will show up at the den of a Bilemaw. Rout the foe, then find a portable stone development in the wall - haul it out and hop up.

Pivot and take out another stone development from the wall and hop over it. Run up the wall to the highest point of the precipice on the right.

Follow the way. Try not to fall into the area covered by blue residue. Take hold of the plants under the roof and move to the metal bar. Then, clutching the edge of the stone rack, move to one side. You will ultimately arrive at a reflection point at the Forest Array.

Utilize the Power on the intuitive component. This will permit Cal to stroll on the metal parts. On the way, you should utilize the Power once more. Arrive at the earthy colored meshes and drop further while hanging down. Move to the top. Here you can open an easy route to the reflection point.

Move along the frameworks to one side. At the point when you arrive at the caught bird, you will fall into the blue residue. You should rapidly get to a protected edge. Proceed and make a wall run. On the way, you can open an entryway and open another easy route.

A Mogu monster will hold you up. In the wake of overcoming the foe, continue to walk and you will arrive at additional earthy colored grates - use them arrive at the highest point of the structure. In the spot displayed in the picture above, you really want to slide down to the round region.

Snatch the sphere and spot it in the speaker, subsequently enacting the laser, which will wear out the entry. There is a reflection point behind the deterrent.

Since the shaft safeguards you from blue residue, you can utilize it to enter another region. Leap to the highest point of the design, where you can initiate another easy route, and afterward leap off the rooftop on the other side.

A direct way will lead you to a limited path, through which you will move tothe Bilemaw Sanctum. You can utilize another contemplation point here.

At the point when you get to an enormous gathering of rivals, you can utilize Befuddle on the Bilemaw to make the battle simpler. At the spot displayed in the picture above, climb the branch and drop down to stay away from the hindrance and continue on.

You will arrive at the slope where you can tame the first relter. You can now utilize these flying birds to fly (you can make slight turns during a flight). At the point when you arrive at the earthy colored grates, get them and move to the rack above. Here you can open the entryway (another alternate route to the contemplation point) or continue right away.

You will get back to the Forest Array. Rout the stormtroopers, then run up the wall toreach the rack with the second relter. Take hold of the animal and fly towards the round square with stormtroopers.

There is another laser, which you can turn utilizing the Power as an afterthought component.

You can alternatively open the way to the main contemplation point or quickly utilize the shaft to obliterate the side obstruction. This will likewise free the huge bird.

At the point when you arrive at the earthy colored grates, climb them to the extremely top. In the long run, you will arrive at the spot with another relter. You arrive where you need to battle more rivals.

Continuing on, you will come to a spot with a circle enhancer. You need to take the sphere from the focal system you used to burst the way to this spot.

Embed the circle in the component and cross the extension to the other stage. Pivot, pull the circle from the primary intensifier and push it towards the second.

You will arrive at a pinnacle with a lift - take it to the extremely top, to the Recovery Wing. At the top, you will find a contemplation point - prepare for a supervisor battle.

After a broad cut-scene, you should confront Dagan, the fourth story supervisor of Star Wars Jedi Survivor. This is a troublesome rival, so you must be exceptionally cautious during the battle. Attempt to repel Dagan's assaults to get him paralyzed - then you will actually want to counterattack.

Leave the Forest Array

Go outside, grab the pipe and go around the top of the tower. Slide down the zipline, grab a relter and soar toward the meditation point.

Check on the Mantis

At this stage, sadly, you can't utilize quick travel to move directly to the Mantis. The way to the principal mission marker prompts the left, along the walls.

You will arrive where you will actually want to tame and ride a Nekko mount.

At the point when you arrive at the primary deterrent, bounce from your mount onto the wall and open the entryway from the other side. En route to the Mantis, you will pass another reflection point.

Meet Cere on Jedha

On this page of our Star Wars Jedi Survivor guide you can find a walkthrough for the Meet Cere on Jedha story mission. We show how and where to find Cere's contact, and how to find the base itself.

Rendezvous with Cere's Contact

In the wake of arriving on Jedha, bounce between stages on the left, then do a wall get and slide down to the stage on the right. From that point, climb the edges up and afterward make a wall run and climb considerably more up. Remember to initiate the alternate route.

You will arrive at a contemplation point. Your objective is a door noticeable somewhere out there, yet getting to it is quite difficult. The sands are home to a beast that will eat Cal assuming he remains on the sandy ground for a

Star Wars Jedi: Survivor: The Complete Official Guide & Walkthrough

really long time. Utilizing rocks and segments, arrive at the entryway and use Power Push to open it.

Go on through the remnants and you'll arrive at an area where you really want to leave the sandy ground as quick as possible to not get eaten. As you circle the point of support with the bar, you'll see a hooking point - use Rising Link. Proceed with the straight way and you'll experience Merrin - a legend you can perceive, as she showed up in the past portion - Star Wars Jedi Fallen Request.

Travel to Cere's Base

Follow Merrin to Cere - at certain minutes, she will make hitches for you to use to get to the upper edges. In the chamber with sculptures, drive the metal component over the slant and use it as a stage to leap to the edge.

You'll experience a foe watch - rout the foes and collaborate with the obliterated vehicle.

As you follow the straight way ahead, you'll arrive where you really want to confront another manager of Star Wars Jedi Survivor. Skriton is a gigantic scorpion that can truly harm his objective with his pliers. During the battle, attempt to remain versatile consistently and evade to circle the supervisor from the left - from that point you can assault and arrangement harm to it. Remember to request Merrin's assistance as frequently as could really be expected - the NIght Sister will nail the beast to the ground with her assaults.

For a more itemized portrayal of the experience, visit a committed page (How to overcome Skriton?).

In the wake of overcoming the chief, tame a Spamel and travel to the mission marker. Eventually you will run into a dust storm and get isolated from Merrin. Search for the partner in the remnants on the left.

Subsequent to finding Merrin, follow the way spread out for you. You will arrive where you will experience some stormtroopers. The crew is joined by a chief - AT-ST. Attempt to draw near to the machine's legs and assault with fast assaults. At the point when the supervisor drops bombs on you, drive them away with Power (they some of the time land back on the adversary).

Star Wars Jedi: Survivor: The Complete Official Guide & Walkthrough

For a more nitty gritty depiction of the experience, visit a devoted page (How to overcome the AT-ST chief?).

In the wake of winning the fight, Merrin will lead you to Cere's refuge. To make the way for the Chronicle, you need to utilize Power to move the circle set apart in the screen capture above. Converse with Cere to close the assignment.

Research Tanalor

Research Tanalor on the Shattered Moon

At the point when you land at the moon base, utilize the close by lift to go down. Proceed to one side, snatch the hooking point, and follow the yellow line and bars to arrive at a contemplation point.

In the wake of entering the structure, continue to walk straight - look out for Clamor Thieves prowling around the bend. Follow the straight way.

You will arrive at the field where you will battle the Reconstructed Magnaguard, one of the supervisors of Star Wars Jedi Survivor. The adversary is quick and forceful, yet he isn't extremely strong - you can continually come down on him to rapidly end the duel.

We portrayed this battle on a different page of this aide: How to overcome Reinvented Magnguard in the Robotized Fashion.

Utilize the Power to incapacitate the impediment on the wall to one side, then get the bars and, keeping away from the power, go as the way leads. This platforming succession is rather extensive - during it you should hop starting with one zipline then onto the next, as well as climb the bars while keeping away from impediments.

You will ultimately arrive at an entryway safeguarded by a green power field. To stay away from the hindrance, follow the way on the right. You will tumble to the base, where you should overcome a few rivals. After the battle, snatch the robot to draw nearer to the bars. Climb them to arrive at the remainder of this area.

Continuing on, you will ultimately arrive at the spot displayed in the picture above. Swing the support utilizing the Power, then move onto it and bounce onto the bars. Then hop towards the rope and get it in flight. Snatching another rope, leap to the stage somewhere far off.

Go into the round room and look at the gadget on the left. You will be gone after by another chief, Drya Thornne. The foe battles with a lightsaber, which he holds with two hands, making his assaults rather sluggish. Significantly, Drya Thornne can become undetectable, yet you will in any case see his framework on the screen - utilize a Power Push to raise a ruckus around town and make him noticeable once more. During the battle, attempt to repel the adversary and assault subsequent to breaking his gatekeeper.

Research Tanalor on Koboh via the Stone Spires

In the wake of arriving on Koboh, follow the way set apart in the picture above. At the point when you arrive at Relter, fly to the cavern inverse. After the reflection point, snatch another Relter and fly through the cavern with magma, utilizing the air current emerging from under the ground.

During the flight you will be gone after by the following manager of Star Wars Jedi Survivor, Korej Lim. The abundance tracker is furnished with a blaster, explosives and a jetpack that keeps him in the air. You want to pull Korej Lim to the cold earth, where he is exposed - the most ideal way to do this is to utilize the manager's projectiles by essentially pushing them back towards him.

Subsequent to winning the fight, gaze upward and climb the wall set apart in the above screen capture. Pushing ahead, rout a few foes and utilize another Relter to arrive at the reflection point.

There is another Relter at the reflection point, however rather than riding it, move in the direction of the support point on the left and leap to get higher. At the top you will track down a sphere speaker. Go past it and enter the cavern on the right.

Go through the hole in the wall in the room and take the square piece off the rack.

Return to the other side of the room, utilize the Power to pivot the instrument and move the laser shaft to the flip side of the space to consume the matter.

Return to the speaker and take out the circle from it, then place it in the connector, admittance to which you have quite recently made. Then, go to the other side of the room, take the sphere from the connector, leave the cavern and spot the circle in the speaker outside.

Star Wars Jedi: Survivor: The Complete Official Guide & Walkthrough

Utilize the sphere speaker to consume matter in the stone beneath. Thusly, you will make an air current that will move you to the following riddle.

Plunge to the reflection point, seize the Relter and utilizing the air current, fly to the stage on the right.

Use Power Pull to uncover the circles connector in the wall. Then, remove the sphere from the speaker and spot it in the connector. You can now continue to the second office of the cavern.

Connect with the machine by the wall to open another capacity for BD-1 called Koboh Processor - the robot can now shoot Koboh matter. Utilize the new capacity to make a string of issue that interfaces the laser pillar to the matter on the wall and continue to the primary room.

Eliminate the circle from the connector and spot it in the speaker. Then, utilize a matter string to interface the two sides of the room with the laser pillar and wear out all the matter.

Climb the wall to the top, then get the sphere from the speaker and put it in the connector on the right wall. Then, run along the wall to the other side, take the circle from the connector and spot it in the sphere speaker outside.

Utilize the circle speaker to consume matter in the stone inverse. Thusly, you will make another air current that will take you to the last riddle.

Fly on the close by Relter into the rising air current and go to the spot set apart in the picture above.

In the cavern you will experience a few Chaos Plunderers. In the wake of overcoming the rivals, utilize the Power and take out a square piece from the wall and afterward block the entryway on the left with it.

Go into the room on the left, take the circle from the connector, go to the fundamental room and spot it in the sphere enhancer. Then, move the square piece so that will obstruct the laser shaft.

Make a string of issue that interfaces the snag on the wall to the laser bar on the solid shape. Then take the sphere from the enhancer and spot it in the one outside.

Utilize the circle speaker to consume off the matter obstructing the last air current, and afterward fly into the Fabulous Yard on a Relter. On the off chance that you should, utilize the contemplation point and plan for a manager battle.

Subsequent to entering the structure, you will be gone after by Tague Louesh, one of the supervisors of Star Wars Jedi Survivor. The rival utilizes a twofold bladed lightsaber, as well as a catching snare, with which he can pull Cal and shock him for a brief time. Attempt to counter your adversary's assaults to break his gatekeeper - then counterattack and go on edge once more.

Subsequent to winning the fight, associate with the gadget lying on the table. To get to the Mantis rapidly, essentially utilize the close by contemplation point and quick travel there.

Reach Pilgrim's Sanctuary

Show Research to Cordova on Jedha

Fly Mantis to the planet Jedha, to Cere's hideout. Open the door to the Archive (push the orb in the vestibule) and talk to Cordova about the devices you found on the Shattered Moon.

Reach Pilgrim's Sanctuary

In the wake of leaving the refuge, get on Spamela. As you stroll through the desert, you will see many side streets, and the way to the mission's really genuine prompts the right, along the wall, at the spot displayed in the picture above.

At the point when you arrive at a cavern with a locked entryway, utilize the Power to drive the stone piece with the rail into place, then push the two circles toward the way to open it. Launch the versatile component out of the wall and use it to leap to the other side.

Proceeding with the principal way, you will arrive at the room displayed in the above screen capture. Utilize the Power to pull the entryway opening instrument.

Go to the entryway, discharge the rope and, utilizing the Power, take out the square piece that will hinder the falling entryway. It will slide the thing under the grille with the instrument - hop higher.

When you are outside, follow the way as displayed in the picture above.

You will arrive at a cliff that you can not get around. Go on through the hole on the left and utilize the Power to pull a metal piece from the wall to impede the breeze. Presently you can leap to the contemplation point.

Continuing on, you should arrive at another metal component you can use to cover yourself from the breeze - you will actually want to move to the remainder of the area.

Where you battle DT Guard Droid, move up the stone support points to the suspended mesh. Move to one side, and toward the finish of the way, drop down to the base. Then, run along the limited wall and get a bar to get around the precarious territory.

You will arrive where you should confront a gathering of rivals. Before you go further, utilize the Power and drive the component into the wall to open the air that will assist you with bouncing further.

At the point when you arrive at the Singing Remains, utilize the Power to pull the two metal shafts (left and right) from the wall - this will permit you to continue to the remainder of this area.

At the point when you slide down the wall to the actual lower part of the room, open the entryway utilizing the Power, hop towards it, and let the breeze convey you to set off a cut-scene. At the point when you gain another expertise, attempt bounce once more to get to the other side.

You will arrive at a scaffold, where you will confront two rivals. Slide down the metal wall to get under the scaffold - follow the straight way.

At the point when you arrive at the spot in the image above, consolidate a twofold leap with a scramble to arrive at the bars. Continuing on, you will arrive at the Pilgrim's Sanctuary and complete this goal.

Locate Brother Armias

Locate Brother Armias

Subsequent to entering the Pilgrim Hallowed place, proceed with the direct way. You are to arrive at an enormous room with additional rivals ultimately. In the wake of managing the stormtroopers, proceed with the way set apart in the picture above - to one side at the green hindrance.

Star Wars Jedi: Survivor: The Complete Official Guide & Walkthrough

Pushing ahead, you are to conquered a few arcade segments. At the point when you arrive at a room with a lake in the center, jump into swim further into the area. You don't need to stress over Cal running out of oxygen.

Burried Refugee puzzle door

When out of the water, get the draping piece on the left and append it to the anchor to eliminate the blockage at the entryway. Then, push with the power half of the entryway on the left side so that it stops on the lock on the right half of the shut door.

Discharge the rope from the anchor, and afterward push the passed on piece of the way to one side, to the lock, to set this piece set up.

At the point when the right 50% of the entryway is toward the finish of the track, utilize the power to pull that part towards you, and around then get the rope on the right side with the ability to move the bar. At the point when the thing is set up, let go of the rope and continue on. Going further you are to arrive at brother Armias.

Bring Contact Codes to Cere

On this page of the guide to Star Wars Jedi Survivor you are to find a walkthrough of the story mission Bring Contact Codes to Cere. You can learn how to pass the arcade sequences and exit the Pilgrim's Sanctuary to reach Cere with the contact codes.

Bring Contact Codes to Cere

After you and Merrin figure out how to escape the imploded burrow, you are to emerged and start taking off from the immense boring machine. As you go through the arcade successions, recollect that tearing through the green power field reestablishes the leap and run (run).

Descending the slant, you should control to the left or right to keep away from the drill and leap out at the perfect locations to try not to fall into the pit.

Follow Merrin through the Pilgrim's Sanctuary. At the point when you arrive at the recently visited room with the green boundary, you are presently ready to get through it. Pushing ahead, you are to confront a grouping of conflicts with additional rivals.

Star Wars Jedi: Survivor: The Complete Official Guide & Walkthrough

When you get to the surface, you start another arcade segment. You are to go through green gateways made by Merrin, consolidating all of this with running on walls and utilizing a rope with a snare.

At the point when you are back on firm ground, help out Merrin (utilize the power) to polish off the penetrating machine. After the fight, play out the last arcade to get to the Contemplation Point.

At this stage, you can just utilize the quick travel choice to move to the Cere base immediately, or traverse the desert to pay attention to more Merrin-related exchange choices.

Rescue Zee from the Lucrehulk

Search for Compass on Koboh

Starting at Cere's base go straight to the planet Koboh to try to find the compass before Dagan Gera. When you land on Koboh, you will trigger a custscene from which you will learn that Zee has been abducted by the Bedlam Raiders.

Rescue Zee from the Lucrehulk

Utilize the quick travel choice and promptly move to the area of the fundamental mission signal. Bounce on the stone point of support with the sphere intensifier, then stroll along the wall to Relter, who will convey you to the perfect locations.

Continuing on, you will arrive at Lucrehulk. Mark the necessary focuses with BD's visor, then take hold of the Relter and fly ahead - you will arrive at a little island in the swamp.

Go to one side, then leap to a low stage drifting in the marsh and pivot. You will see a way under the island - head down that path. Further on, you will confront a short arcade grouping and a battle with a few rivals, until you at long last arrive at the reflection point.

Ask Bode for help to dump the compartment into the swamp. Along these lines, you will make an extension empowering you to cross to the other side. Proceeding with the direct way and finishing more arcade segments, you will ultimately arrive at the reflection point in the shed (Overhang Rafters).

The street go on through the green power field on the left. To play it as protected as possible conceivable, you can run along the wall on the left and leap to the overhang on the right. Then hang tight for the right second and run up the wall on the option to get around the power field as the electric snare goes off for some time.

Continuing on, you will ultimately arrive at the spot displayed in the screen capture over (the hall on the right prompts an easy route to the contemplation point). Get around the bars, and from that point, getting through the power field, hop into the room with a few foes.

Follow Bode along the direct way until you arrive at the following contemplation point. Proceed with the way set apart in the screen capture above. Sooner or later, a gun dangling from the roof will start taking shots at you - you can't obliterate it as of now. Go ahead, redirecting the turret blaster fire (look out for the Pandemonium Thief sneaking around the bend) and follow the way on the right.

Further to one side, you should get around a hole to arrive on the stage underneath. Go through the power field, rout the rivals, and progress forward as the way leads.

Take a run-up, leap to the getting holder and stumbled into it, then run forward and utilize the catching snare, with the goal that you land at your objective.

Keep investigating until you arrive at the Yurt Barracs. The right way prompts the left. Continuing on, you will arrive at the second piece of the structures, where significantly more adversaries are positioned.

At the point when the battle is finished, ask Bode to drop the rope, on which you will rise to a higher floor. Be ready to battle a ton of rivals who will go after in waves.

Eventually, you will be gone after by Rayvis. Nonetheless, the battle won't occur, and you will slide down the wall to the lower part of the shed. Evade the turret blaster fire for some time. From that point forward, a cutscene will be set off, during which you will master new abilities: Liftand Hammer.

Utilizing your recently gained capacities, return to the highest point of the shed, to the contemplation point at the Lucrehulk Center. En route, you will confront a more drawn out arcade grouping.

Inverse the reflection point is a lift. Utilizing your recently obtained power, you can now bring it and take it up the mountain.

At the point when you arrive at the Forward Control Pinnacle, utilize the contemplation point and get ready for a supervisor battle. Follow the way to one side, at the spot set apart in the screen capture above.

This will be the second time you should battle Dagan Gera. During this conflict, Dagan will display new mechanics and assaults. Make a point to act protectively and attempt to break his watchman to bring out a few precise assaults.

Locate Rayvis on the Shattered Moon

On this guide page to Star Wars Jedi Survivor, you will find a walkthrough of the story mission Locate Rayvis on the Shattered Moon. You will learn how to pass the challenging arcade sections, solve the puzzle with the Orb Amplifier, and get to Rayvis.

Locate Rayvis on the Shattered Moon

In the wake of arriving on the Shattered Moon, go down to the Contemplation Point and utilize the quick travel - move close to the principal mission marker. Go up the incline and, utilizing the Power, open the entry on the right.

Utilizing the rope, leap to a more elevated level, trust that the laser will switch off, and afterward leap to the other side of the room. Sit tight for the right second and bounce onto the getting stage when the laser turns off and quickly leap to the bars. Then, enter the laser burrow when it is idle and hurried to the subsequent room, where you will go through another arcade arrangement.

You will arrive at a room where you will meet a various foe crew. You can utilize the laser during battle, as it harms all objectives inside its reach.

You should go through the continuous arcade areas. Going through another passage with a laser bar, you will ultimately arrive at a little room on the left. Obliterate the thin impediment to continue on. At last you will arrive at a contemplation point.

Go to the patio, hop into the room on the left, and rout a few rivals.

Utilize the Power to get the Circle you track down in the space on the other side of the glass. Then, push it toward the wall on the left so it starts moving down the stage.

Move somewhat to one side and catch the Sphere with the Power before it falls into the chasm. Position the person in a manner that permits you to push the Sphere to move down the stage on the right.

Promptly rush to the room on the other side of the entryway and attempt to get the Orbbefore it falls into the pit.

Place it in the enhancer to enact the laser. Utilizing the BD-1 capacity, make a line of issue driving from the hindrance to the laser pillar to open the section.

Communicate with the workbench in the round space to set off a cutscene, during which you will get a Redesigned Climb Link.

From here on out, you can get inflatables in the air and skip off them to arrive at beforehand distant spots. At the point when you arrive at the spot displayed in the image above, skip off the inflatable on the left to get to the one on the right, from which you can bob toward the wall on the left and hop higher.

Utilize the control center to enact the inflatables, then hop between them to get to the pinnacle, where you will battle against a chief.

Another manager you experience in the Star Wars Jedi Survivor game is Rayvis. The battle against this rival is separated into two stages. Rayvis is an imposing rival, particularly on higher trouble levels, so we exhort playing protectively, hindering customary assaults (as frequently as your block bar will permit you to do) to intrude on the manager's assault. Look out for red assaults - evade them and convey a blow when the rival stops.

Confront Dagan at the Koboh Observatory

BD-1 Electro Dart

Subsequent to arriving on Koboh, open the guide and follow the way set apart in the image above. Strolling to one side, you will ultimately arrive at a green power field - keep strolling that way until you arrive at the Misted Span area.

You will get to a consuming region - a position of a boat crash. Rout the rivals positioned there, then snatch the catch, bounce higher, and enter the disaster area.

Slither through the boat and, toward its finish, you will open the BD-1 Electro Dart expertise.

From here onward, you can utilize the new capacity to over-burden specific articles, consequently opening up already distant courses.

Confront Dagan at the Koboh Observatory

At the point when you arrive at the Reflection Point (Hazed Breadth), enter the cabin at the top and bounce onto the stage on the right.

Utilize the Power to open a window in the room, then go through it and bring down back.

Remaining on the lower level, utilize the BD-1 Electro Dart to over-burden the item and move the wall on the right, which you will use to get to the other side - start running when the wall is returning to the starting position.

Continuing on, you will ultimately arrive at the spot displayed in the image above. You should confront three influxes of foes. Adversaries will likewise go after from galleries on the two sides.

After the battle, take the lift up, and utilize a psyche stunt on the Stormtrooper to inspire him to open the entryway for you. Keep strolling the hallway, then use BD-1 Electro Dart to make a section. Follow the direct way.

Utilize the Power to haul the inflatable out of the machine on the right and position it so you can leap to the closest stage. Hop between stages on the inflatables until you arrive at the Observatory.

Go into the oval room through a hole in the wall. When inside, use BD-1 Electro Dart to over-burden the circuit in the room behind the glass and open the seal.

Head outside, make a beeline for the right and hop into the room through the recently opened hatch. Make the way for let the laser pillar through to the principal room, then make a way of issue from the hindrance to the laser.

Get an inflatable from the gadget here, move it outside, and position it so you can leap to the following stage. Arrive at the upper level to the Reflection Point, and afterward keep going the straight way.

Utilize the BD-1 Electro Dart to move the wall somewhat higher. Then, run along the wall and utilize a scramble toward the finish to fall on the matrix and turn it.

Get around the following moving wall so as to move in the direction of the wall and move up it.

Bouncing between the launchers on the arms of the pivoting propeller, circumvent the obstruction from the right side.

At the point when you pass through the locked entryway, you will confront a smaller than usual chief - Urgost, Clench hand of Rayvis. This is a customary rival with no extra assaults. Urgost is extremely sluggish, so basically keep away from his blows and immediately counterattack as well as repel his ordinary assaults.

In the wake of winning the fight, utilize the BD-1 Electro Dart to open the entryway. Then, actuate the arm with the inflatables and utilize one of them to bounce onto the contrary stage.

At the point when you're on the other side, actuate the arm once more so you can utilize the inflatables. Position the inflatable so you can hop onto the stage above.

You will arrive at a room where you will see pivoting walls. Snatch the one nearest to you, then wall-run counterclockwise and bounce between the ensuing walls. You will arrive at a reflection point.

Communicate with the terminal in the following area to open a roundabout room with two foes. After the battle, use BD-1 Electro Dart to turn this room.

You will be gone after by a few foes. Subsequent to winning the fight, utilize the Electro Dart once more and turn the room.

Indeed you will be gone after. In the room you recently opened, you will see a gadget with inflatables - leave it for the present and turn the room once more.

Presently you will approach both the room with the inflatable and the section to the other piece of this area. Take an inflatable and position it in such a manner you can leap to the mesh. Follow the direct way.

At the point when you arrive at the contemplation point, rest and get ready to meet the chief, Dagan Gera. This time Bode will help you in the battle, and the fight is separated into 4 stages. The strategies are equivalent to during past conflicts with Dagan.

Bring Compass to Cordova on Jedha

Bring Compass to Cordova on Jedha

After landing at the base on Jeda, go straight to the archives and hand the compass to Cordova. After the cutscene, go check the progress made by the NPC.

Pursue Bode

At the point when the following cut scene is finished, set off in quest for Bode - up the lift and afterward to the carport, where a speeder will be hanging tight for you.

Follow Bode through the Jedha desert, keeping away from hindrances. You will at last raise a ruckus around town , where you should confront the double crosser, however at this stage you can not complete the rival and the battle will be halted when Bode gets sufficient harm.

Stall the Empire's Assault

You will assume the job of Cere and should attempt to stop the attack. Manage all adversaries, then move towards the base.

Follow Merrin through the base, dispensing with any foes experienced en route. At the point when you get outside, climb the slope utilizing stones.

Utilize the Power to move the circle in the wall - this will set off a component that will drop a bomb on the attack machines. Then, go through the cavern (the entry was uncovered after the bomb was dropped) to the top and drop another bomb.

Reach the Hangar

Star Wars Jedi: Survivor: The Complete Official Guide & Walkthrough

Request that Merrin hurl down the rope and climb, then move down the wall to the storage. At the point when you arrive at the Documents, utilize the contemplation point and plan for a supervisor battle.

The following manager in Star Wars Jedi Survivor is Darth Vader, and the duel has been partitioned into 3 phases. Vader is slow, however he can cause a great deal of harm rapidly, so you must be cautious constantly, repel standard catastrophes for break your rival's watchman and stay away from red assaults.

Locate Bode

Locate Bode

Subsequent to landing, leave the Mantis and utilize the electric dart to open the entryway. Continuing on, you will arrive at a red power field - you can enter it by running through it, similarly as with the green hindrances.

Follow the direct way until you arrive at an impasse - slice through the upward pipes in one of the rooms to continue on. Utilize the electric dart to draw the arm nearer, after which you can bounce into the room behind the red hindrance.

Leave the room and, utilizing the bar, hop higher, then open the entryway and utilize the electric dart to move the arm to the other side. Presently you can hop into the room on the contrary side of the shed. Follow the straight way.

At the point when you arrive at the Headquarters, all ways out will be impeded. Utilize the Power to uncover the component and use BD-1's electric dart to open the entry.

Go to Bode's Quarters

Whenever you arrive at the spot displayed in the screen capture , you should go through the focal alternating purpose in the room, keeping away from the red walls or running through themand snatching the snares on the right side. Then hop between stages to get to the top.

You will arrive at a hall that is safeguarded by a moving red power field. Take out the adversaries and go into the room on the left, utilize the electric dart, and afterward bounce higher through the shaft in the roof.

Subsequent to entering Bode's quarters, you should get some data. Actually take a look at the accompanying things in the room:

- A base of pillows and blankets,

- Datapad on the table,

- A painting on the wall (by the table, facing the bedroom).

Open the bedroom door and take the datadisk, which lies on the seat to the left. Exit the bedroom and interact with the desktop in the middle of the room to activate the cutscene.

Pursue Bode

You will currently confront a more drawn out grouping of battles with different rivals, who will show up in waves. In the end, you will arrive at the shed, where you should confront significantly more adversaries coming in waves. After the battle, make a beeline for Mantis.

Align Arrays at Koboh Control Center

This page of the guide to Star Wars Jedi Survivor includes a walkthrough of the story mission Align Arrays at Koboh Control Center. You will learn how to reach the control room and how to open the passage leading to Tanalor.

Align Arrays at Koboh Control Center

Subsequent to arriving on Koboh, make a beeline for the entry set apart in the screen capture above. Head inside and bring the lift down into the mountain.

Subsequent to battling a few influxes of foes, go on through the entryway. At the point when you arrive at the terminal, actuate it to stop the pivoting rings. Then utilize the Power to make a scaffold.

Go to the control center and interface with the control board on the option to start the lift and go higher. At the point when you arrive at the top, collaborate with the terminal again to finish the responsibility.

Confront Bode on Tanalorr

Star Wars Jedi: Survivor: The Complete Official Guide & Walkthrough

This page of the guide to Star Wars Jedi Survivor describes the story mission titled Confront Bode on Tanalorr. This is a very short mission where you will explore a bit of Tanalorr and face the final story-related boss in Star Wars Jedi Survivor.

Confront Bode on Tanalorr

In the wake of arriving on Tanalor, follow the straight way with Merrin. The street leads across the water and afterward to one side, between the stones.

Following the straight way, you will arrive at the Sanctuary Chamber. In the event that you should, utilize the reflection point and offer all your ability focuses, in light of the fact that you are going to battle the last manager in Star Wars Jedi Survivor.

After a more extended cutscene, you will start the last fight with Bode. The last conflict is separated into 3 sections, and in the initial segment you can utilize Merrin's assistance. Bode is incredibly coordinated, and he joins his blows into destructive mixes, so you must be exceptionally cautious and attempt to get through his safeguards, which will empower you to convey a few precise blows.

Secrets and Collectibles

Unique Collectibles

Stim Canisters

One of the main types of secrets in Star Wars Jedi Survivor are chests with stim canisters. Our collectibles guide will help you find them. Each of them can permanently increase the number of healing charges by 1.

Coruscant #1 - Undercity Meats

A chest with a stim canister is in Undercity Meats. You'll arrive at this area after your most memorable experience with the 10th Sister (the one where you don't battle her yet).

Arrive at the contemplation point in Undercity Meats. You will find an upward climbing wallnext to it. At the top you need to manage a huge droid. The chest is close to an enormous red turbine.

Koboh #1 - Doma's Outpost Commodities

Star Wars Jedi: Survivor: The Complete Official Guide & Walkthrough

On Koboh, you really want to arrive at the Drifter's Arrive at Station - you will open Doma's Station Wares. Purchase the Baffling Keycode - it costs 10 priorite shards. You need to track down these fortunes in the game world (one of the collectibles).

The Secretive Keycode opens a side room in the store. There is a chest with a stim canister in it.

Koboh #2 - Foothill Falls

The mysterious chest is located in the Lower region Falls locale, which you can reach from the Drifter's Arrive at Station. You really want to arrive at the area displayed in the photos above. You will initially open the Relter Tame ability in the primary storyline. Snatch a relter and you will arrive at a region with a blue cottage - the collectible is inside it. Rout a gathering of rivals in the new area.

Admittance to the collectible is impeded by a fragile construction that can't be obliterated by customary techniques.

Investigate the region to find a nekko mount. Return to the hovel and sling yourself together with the nekko toward the running wall. You will arrive at a higher rack with it.

Utilize the bar to leap to the other side. When you are on the new rack, BD-1 can hack the terminal - rollers mine might show up. You really want to rapidly get a mine with the Power and toss it at the opening on the top of the cottage with the mystery (point somewhat higher). After a few endeavors, you will obliterate the delicate construction.

You can now return ground floor and visit the private alcoves of the cottage. There is a chest with a stim canister.

Koboh #3 - Basalt Rift

The secret chest is on one of the hills in the Basal Rift region. The enemies you encounter along the way can be avoided.

Koboh #4 - Viscid Bog

The chest with a Max Stims Increased upgrade is on one of the islets. There is also a large opponent (The Mirre Terror) that you will have to defeat before opening the chest.

Koboh #5 - Observatory Understructure

From the spot where the Observatory Understructure region starts, go to one side to climb walls. You will get to the stage with an electric obstruction on the right side. There, leap to the climbing wall utilizing the launcher on the enormous turning structure.

Once at the top, go through the hole on the left. There, get an inflatable and throw it outside - in the wake of hopping on it, quickly pivot to hop a level higher.

Subsequent to landing, you will track down a chest.

Jedha #1 - Sheltered Hollow

The chest with the stim canister is in a cave in Sheltered Hollow, near the meditation point. You have to pass through this area in the main storyline on your way to the Cere base. This makes the secret hard to miss.

Jedha #2 - Crypt of Uhrma

The Stim Canister is in the shut piece of the Sepulcher of Uhrma, a discretionary area gave the way to the Pilgrim's Sanctuary on Jedha later in the mission.

We depicted how to open the grave on a different page The riddle of opening the Sepulcher of Uhrma on Jedha.

Shattered Moon #1 - Assembly Staging

This is a hazardous collectible, since it drives you to arrive along the edge region of the Gathering Organizing displayed in the image. You can gain from one of the NPCs about the chance of examining it and opening a discretionary Talk (not expected to get the mystery).

You should start in the fundamental piece of the locale and utilize the climbing walls and running walls from picture 1. You will arrive where you need to slide down the rope. Land on the edge from picture 2, yet solely after Cal is near it (a tumble from level could kill him).

In an enormous heater like area, arrive at another line and watch out for releases while utilizing it (picture 1). You will arrive at a rack with a yellow chest containing a Stim Canister - a super durable increment of BD-1's mending charges by 1.

Information on finding Stim Canisters

Stim canisters are, as we would like to think, the main classification of collectibles. They are put away in enormous yellow chests, which you can open with BD-1's assistance.

Each stim canister obtained will build the quantity of mending charges by 1. This is exceptionally useful particularly during supervisor battles - you will actually want to mend more times during a battle. Toward the start of the game you have just 2 recuperating charges.

You can recharge your spent stims by utilizing the rest choice at reflection focuses. You ought to go with a full inventory as frequently as could be expected.

Map Updates

The universes and planets of Star Wars Jedi Survivor are filled to the edge with collectibles and mysteries. To make thinking that they are more straightforward, you can acquire Guide Updates, which generally, are treasure maps. From this page of our aide, you'll figure out how and where to get updates that mark explicit kinds of privileged insights - Data sets, Fortunes, Collectible Chests, Seedbags, and Substances. Also, we make sense of how for utilize these redesigned maps.

Upgrade #1 - Database

In the first place, you want to progress in the principal story enough to open Nova Garon. In the Headquarters area, you'll be exposed to a cut-scene portraying the conflict with Denvik. After the cut-scene, don't leave the room yet and search for an intelligent terminal. BD-1 will download a guide with areas of all Data sets (reverberations and readable items).

Upgrade #2 - Chest

This one must be gotten after the finish of the fundamental story. On Koboh, you want to visit Phon'Qi Sinkholes and rout 3 small scale supervisors there. At the point when the region is clear, move toward the intelligent terminal. Cooperate with it and BD-1 will download a guide with the areas of all Chests (counting those that contain the most significant Stim Canisters).

Opening admittance to the caverns and crossing them is depicted on a different page - Arriving at the Phon'Qi Caves.

Upgrade #3 - Treasure

This one must be gotten after the finish of the primary story. In the world Jedha, you should open admittance to the Wayfinder's Burial place nearby the Parched Pads district. This includes going through 3 other discretionary areas with natural riddles. More data can be tracked down on a different page - Wayfinder's Burial place.

There is an intelligent terminal in the burial place. Communicate with it and BD-1 will download a guide with all Fortunes stamped (Priorite Shards, Datadiscs, and Jedha Parchments).

Upgrade #4 - Essence

This one can only be gotten after the end of the main story. In addition, you must complete all 7 Jedi Chambers, which are optional locations with altars. We described the chambers and their exploration in the Puzzles chapter:

- Chamber of Duality;

- Chamber of Reason;

- Chamber of Fortitude;

- Chamber in the Devastated Settlement;

- Chamber of Detachment;

- Chamber of Connection;

- Chamber of Clarity.

After completing the last seventh chamber, you should unlock the Star Tours trophy - a sign that you can focus on the next step.

In the world Koboh you need to arrive at the Alignment Control Center - it is close to the Drifter's Arrive at Station which you visit in the principal storyline.

Close to the reflection point are 7 posts. All screens ought to shine green to affirm that you have finished the Jedi chambers. Red variety implies that some chamber was not gotten done, for example you didn't take the advantage from its special raised area.

Turn 180 degrees. You can inspect the intelligent terminal. BD-1 can download from it a guide with the areas of all embodiments (they are called redesigns).

Upgrade #5 - Seedbag

On Jedha, travel to Stormy Plateau and quest for Pili Walde - subsequent to enlisting this person, she will deal with the nursery on the top of Saloon. Converse with her about it.

Presently you should find somewhere around 1 seedbag of each kind (on the whole, there are 10 of them). Convey 10 unique seedbags to Pyloon's Cantina on Koboh. You can utilize them to develop plants on the roof garden (some time should elapse before they sprout).

At last, you'll open admittance to an intuitive terminal. Interface with it for BD-1 to download a guide denoting the areas of all seedbags.

How Map Upgrades work

With each Map Upgrade received, the Holomap will mark all collectibles of the given type. This applies also to the regions you haven't visited yet. Using treasure maps is very useful when attempting to get the missed secrets and attain 100% completion of a region.

Mysterious Keycode

Purchasing the Mysterious Keycode

On your most memorable visit toKoboh , you will visit Drifter's Arrive at Station and in the wake of meeting Greez, Doma's Station Wares store will be opened.

One of the things in Doma's stock is the Mysterious Keycode.

Sadly, to get it, you really want Priorite Shards. Shards are one of the kinds of collectibles and you can track down them on the planet among Fortunes - search for gleaming items.

Gather somewhere around 10 Priorite Shards and use them to purchase the mysterious keycode.

Using Mysterious Keycode

With the Keycode, BD-1 can now open a side door of the store.

Behind the door, you'll encounter a large chest containing a Stim Canister. This is a very valuable find, as it increases the number of carried Stims by 1.

Force Tears

Tear #1 - Fractured Malice

Location: Coruscant - Rooftops

Depiction: Tear #1 is in a little room experienced toward the start of the housetops segment. This tear must be finished subsequent to learning Power Lift and opening Coruscant as an objective. Force Lift the entryway to track down the Tear.

This challenge is truly challenging, as the need might arise to overcome 2 Rancors in a single battle. This implies twofold the test (in the event that one Malignity wasn't sufficient) and to endure you really want to respond in a split second to risky assaults coming from the two monsters. Most importantly, try not to get assaults that can destroy you in a split second. Assault and dispose of the monsters individually. Prior to actuating the Tear, you can bring down the trouble level, which brings about lower strength and less soundness of the rivals.

Tear #2 - Fractured Resolve

Location: Koboh - Swindler's Wash

Description: Once in this region, follow the riverbed. Eventually you will reach a waterfall and the Tear is behind it.

The challenge takes a form of a obstacle course, where the safe path changes with each jump. Play it safe - there is no time limit that forces you to rush the course. If necessary, change the incoming wave to a safe one (jump) and wait for it to pass Cal.

Tear #3 - Fractured Tradition

Location: Jedha - Monastery Walls

Depiction: Start at the reflection point. You want to get to the furthest left piece of the vestiges, get a hitch while sliding down a lofty slant and bounce from one segment to another (screen capture).

You will ultimately arrive at an upper rack in the vestiges and this is where you track down the Tear.

The test of Tear #3 includes overcoming a gathering of foes while utilizing Single position - you can't change to other positions all through the term of the test. Luckily, you will not need to confront any tip top adversaries here, however make sure to keep away from red assaults and use repel.

Tear #4 - Fractured Determination

Location: Jedha - Desert Ridge

Portrayal: Start with finding the green entryway concealed in the stone arrangements - to have the option to get to its other side, you want to open Merrin's Appeal in the principal story. The actual Tear is in a little cavern.

The test includes finishing a troublesome hindrance course in which you want to air run through series of green doors (some of them are moving) and perform wall runs. Remember that your moves' cooldowns are renewed with each passing of a green door, so you can utilize hops and runs endlessly. There are some resting spots en route. Utilize the break and trust that the entryways will align well or for the electric snares to move away.

Tear #5 - Fractured Dexterity

Location: Jedha - Blustery Mesa

Portrayal: Not a long way from the boundary with Trailhead Pantheon, you'll find an area with solid breeze blasts and a region reasonable for a wall run. Arrive at the lower hallways to track down a green door (to have the option to get to its other side, you really want to advance in the principal

Star Wars Jedi: Survivor: The Complete Official Guide & Walkthrough

story enough to get Merrin's Appeal). Subsequent to moving beyond the entryway, you'll end up in a grave with the Tear.

The test includes overcoming a gathering of foes while utilizing Double Use position - you can't change the position all through the length of the test. There will be additional approaching rivals, however they will just show up subsequent to overcoming all or the greater part of the ongoing gathering. At last, you'll need to confront a marginally more grounded monster.

Tear #6 - Fractured Cunning

Location: Jedha - Timeworn Bridge

Portrayal: Start from the contemplation point, then continue to the principal climbing way. En route, you ought to experience a green door (to have the option to get to its other side, you really want to advance in the fundamental story enough to get Merrin's Appeal). The Tear is on the other side of a laser entryway.

The test requires overcoming a gathering of rivals while utilizing Blaster position - you need to remain with this position all through the span of the test. There will be additional approaching rivals, however they will just show up subsequent to overcoming all or a large portion of the ongoing gathering. Luckily, no first class foes will enter the scene.

Tear #7 - Fractured Endurance

Location: Destroyed Moon - Automated Forge

Portrayal: In the wake of arriving at the manufacture, go to the room where you've battled Magnaguard. In the following room go with the ascension (and keep away from traps en route) or get the rope in the event that you've opened the alternate way before. Nearby from screen capture 1, you want to snatch the bar and stay away from the last snares. You will arrive at the room with the Tear.

The test sees you annihilate 150 fight droids. Consider utilizing Twofold Bladed position to effectively dispatch adversaries more. Try to reflect blaster shots and in the further piece of the fight, keep away from projectiles by avoiding their impact range.

Tear #8 - Fractured Burden

Location: Koboh - Gorge Crash Site

Portrayal: Start at the contemplation point and search for a lift. Enter the lift and leap out of it immediately so it rides up void. Where the lift was, you can utilize Power Hammer however provided that you've opened this power in the primary storyline. Hop down to the lower region - the Tear is there.

The test includes overcoming 3 minibosses, and these are all the more impressive variations of monsters that you've had the valuable chance to experience during investigation. Rout the foes individually, however look out for assaults from residual adversaries. Likewise, keep an eye out for red assaults which come in various renditions, as you're confronting monsters of various types.

Tear #9 - Fractured Agility

Location: Koboh - Derelict Dam

Depiction: The way to this Tear leads through a discretionary Bubbling Feign district. Use Nekko to arrive at one of the upper racks. There you'll track down an intuitive station (screen capture 1). Assume the inflatable and position it above Cal. You can now snatch it and use it to sling yourself to the following inflatables. To have the option to play out that activity, you want to have updated Rising Link, which is opened after sufficient advancement in the fundamental storyline.

At long last, Cal will arrive on a rack before a huge bird who you had liberated before. Communicate with the bird - it will take Cal to an alternate area.

You'll wind up on the most noteworthy racks of the Forsaken Dam locale (in the meantime, you can alternatively open an easy route - a lift). Check out the area to track down the Tear.

The test of this Tear includes finishing a troublesome snag course which requires putting inflatables, joining to them, and performing wall runs. You should try not to contact red obstructions and other hindrances. Rehash the test until you have it dominated. Recollect that when on an inflatable, you can hold the button to defer and design the heading of the catapulting prior to taking the leap.

Tear #10 - Fractured Momentum

Location: Koboh - Smuggler's Tunnels

Portrayal: Start at the bar reflection point and pick the way to Bootlegger's Passages. En route through this district, you should move beyond a green door twice and this requires Merrin's Appeal, a thing got over the principal storyline. The subsequent green entryway is arrived at through a wall run. Search for the Tear on the other side.

The test of this Tear includes finishing a troublesome impediment course during which you'll pass green boundaries (at times in mid-air) and get ropes. Keep an eye out for traps and red boundaries. Keep in mind, likewise, that your moves' cooldowns are recharged after each passing of a green boundary, so you can fire your leaps and runs immediately once more.

Tear #11 - Fractured Delusion

Location: Koboh - Hunter's Quarry

Portrayal: Getting to this Tear requires some planning. Start at Drifter's Arrive at Station and track down a locked constructing (screen capture 1). You need to open it by utilizing Power Pull, BD-1 hacking, Power Hammer (power acquired over the story), and Merrin's Appeal. At the point when you'll at long last move beyond the entryway, you'll track down Soont Madas inside. Converse with him and use Brain Control on him (pick any discourse choice you like). Get to the cellar and explore the carcass. While endeavoring to get back higher up, Soont Madas will go after Cal. You need to overcome him - this is likewise a first experience with another sort of rival.

Back at Drifter's Arrive at Outpost, you really want to move to the top of Doma's store. Continue to the climbable wall from screen capture 2.

You will get yourself high over the Tracker's Quarry district. There are intelligent inflatables here and you can contact them gave you have redesigned Rising Link which is opened with sufficient advancement in the fundamental storyline. Arrive at the inflatable displayed in screen capture 1 - launch, play out a wall run and arrive at a little cavern that contains the Tear.

The actual test is straightforward and includes overcoming a gathering of rivals. There will be additional approaching adversaries, however they will just show up subsequent to overcoming all or the greater part of the ongoing gathering.

Tear #12 - Fractured Duality

Location: Koboh - Rambler's Reach Outpost

Portrayal: Get to the nursery on the saloon's rooftop. There is a pinnacle close to it and you can move up the wall displayed in screen capture 1. Advance toward the highest point of the pinnacle - there you'll track down the Tear.

The test includes overcoming a gathering of rivals utilizing Twofold Bladed position - you need to remain with a similar position all through the entire battle or the test will be fizzled. Make a point to divert shots from weighty cannons with your lightsaber, and look out for red assaults from droids.

Tear #13 - Fractured History

Location: Koboh - Rambler's Reach Outpost

Description: the path to this Tear leads through an optional Fort Kah'lin region. Reach its upper levels and enter the arena where you need to face Spawn of Oggdo boss.

After defeating the boss, you need to perform 2 interactions:

- Investigate the echo of the first small oggdo encountered in the same area i.e. the boss's lair (screenshot 1).

- Investigate the echo of the second small oggdo encountered in Doma's shop in Rambler's Reach Outpost (screenshot 2). The blue glow will appear only if you've investigated the first oggdo.

With the second oggdo researched, the Tear will show up in Doma's store. Your undertaking in this challenge will be to overcome a couple of Oggdos. The battle is extremely difficult, as the need might arise to keep an eye out and respond to assaults from two foes simultaneously. Most importantly, keep an eye out for red assaults which are getting endeavors that when success in enormous harm got. Assault and take out the monsters individually. Prior to enacting the Tear, you can bring down the trouble level, which brings about lower strength and less soundness of the rivals.

Tear #14 - Fractured Punishment

Location: Koboh - Devastated Settlement

Portrayal: Start by arriving at Amazing Yard reflection point (this point is opened with progress in the principal story) located on the most elevated floor of Crushed Settlement. Look at the racks close to the contemplation point, and you ought to see an enormous solid shape (screen capture 1). The Tear is inside it, and you can arrive at it by utilizing a relter.

The related test is rather straightforward - you really want to overcome a gathering of monsters. Luckily, there aren't any world class beasts here, yet make sure to keep away from red assaults.

Tear #15 - Fractured Power

Location: Koboh - Marl Cavern

Depiction: The way to this Tear leads through the Hazed Breadth district. Either complete a more extended climb and arrive at the principal access to the cavern (screen capture 1) or utilize the easy route close to the contemplation point in the event that you've opened it before.

Inside the cavern, you'll have to do some wall runs and arrive at the inflatable (screen capture 2). For this you want overhauled Climb Link which is opened with sufficient advancement in the primary storyline.

Launch yourself from the inflatable toward the rack.

The test of this Tear includes overcoming a gathering of rivals utilizing Crossguard position - you can't change to other positions all through the term of the test or it will be fizzled. There will be additional approaching rivals, however they will just show up subsequent to overcoming all or a large portion of the ongoing gathering. At long last, there are 2 bigger monsters to overcome, however they are not undeniable supervisors.

Force Tears - general info

On the whole, there are 15 Power Tears to find and finish in Jedi Survivor. This is one of the main classifications of collectibles, and there is a special test related with each Tear. It very well may be a battle challenge that includes overcoming managers or gatherings of foes, or a deterrent course.

Finishing a Tear is compensated with 1 Expertise Point. Besides, for finishing every one of the 15, you'll open a gold prize - Hard labor.

Coming to and finishing Tears might require specific contraptions or capacities for example overhauled Climb Link, Merrin's Appeal, or Power Hammer capacity. It is ideal to stand by with finishing them until the principal story is finished.

All fish

Finding and recruiting Skoova the fisherman

Gathering one of a kind types of fish is one of the discretionary exercises in the game. It isn't accessible all along of the mission. You should initially find and enroll the fisherman Skoova and really at that time will it become conceivable to look for the 12 types of fish, which are treated as collectibles.

Skoova is in the Lower region Falls district on Koboh and you can arrive from the Drifter's Arrive at Station. Converse with Skoova and enroll him to the saloon. From this point forward you can likewise experience Skoova in the game world. Converse with him whenever you get an opportunity and he will get every one of the 12 fish for Cal. You can arrive at the fishing grounds in any request.

Fish #1 - See Fish

Location: Koboh - Foothill Falls

You can unlock the fish in the same place where you met Skoova. Talk to him again to catch it.

Fish #2 - Barbed Hookfish

Location: Koboh - Smuggler's Tunnels

Here you must reach the main underground water reservoir.

Fish #3 - Big-Mouth Faa

Location: Koboh - Rift Passage

This is a small region visited in the main storyline - you will find Skoova right next to the meditation point.

Fish #4 - Blinding Rayfish

Location: Koboh - Devastated Settlement

The fishery is on a rocky shelf surrounded on all sides by precipices. You have to use a relter to get there.

Fish #5 - Blue-Finned Crayfish

Location: Koboh - Bygone Settlement

The fishery is located next to a steep slope leading to the neighboring Nekko Pools region.

Note - If the interaction with Skoova does not become available then reload the game or use fast travel to reload Koboh.

Fish #6 - Fantailed Laa

Location: Jedha - Crypt of Uhrma

You will track down the fishery behind the tomb. You should initially open the enormous door in it. The answer for the riddle in the Sepulcher of Uhrma is portrayed on a different page of the aide. Skoova is remaining close to where you can open one of the easy routes.

Fish #7 - Fingerlip Garpon

Location: Koboh - Rambler's Reach Outpost

Skoova moored the boat at a river located on the outskirts of the settlement.

Fish #8 - Frilled Newt

Location: Koboh - Gorge Crash Site

You can find Skoova's boat a short distance from the meditation point.

Fish #9 - Glottsamcrab

Location: Koboh - Viscid Bog

Skoova's boat is moored at one of the rock ledges in the swamp. Don't jump into the bog - you can get the fish by staying on stable ground.

Fish #10 - Mee Fish

Location: Koboh - Mountain Ascent

You can reach Skoova after going through the green gates on the way to the observatory (you need to unlock Merrin's Charm first).

Fish #11 - Snakefish

Location: Jedha - Arid Flats

You will find a small body of water by the rocks near one of the meditation points.

Fish #12 - Viscid Lurker

Location: Koboh - Phon'Qi Caverns

The method for finding this mysterious area is depicted on the page Arriving at Phon'Qi Cavernsin the Riddles section. Skoova is remaining at one of the most reduced levels of the caverns.

Aquarium for caught fish

The main reward for finding all 12 fish is a silver Skoova Diving trophy.

You can moreover visit the Pyloon's Cantina. Head higher up and you'll find an enormous aquarium where the examples you catch can show up. You can converse with Skoova here, as well as inspect the aquarium from the other side and really take a look at a rundown of gotten fish (it's an effective method for following advancement).

Coruscant

Rooftops

List of Rooftops secrets

There are 6 collectibles:

- Chest: 2
- Databank: 2
- Force Tear: 1
- Treasure: 1

Chest #1

The chest is easy to find - just after reaching the Rooftops for the first time. This will occur shortly after confronting the senator and climbing.

The chest contains a lightsaber part.

Chest #2

You will find the chest in a side region close to the main reflection point. Start at the contemplation point and request that BD-1 hack the entryway. Additionally utilize the Power to close the huge seal en route. This will empower you to arrive at the last rack with the collectible.

The chest contains a lightsaber part.

Databank #1 - Abandoned Squatter Site

The collectible is in the location with the first meditation point. You will find it in a dark corner.

Databank #2 - Squatter Camp

You will find the secret in an abandoned camp, where, after climbing, Cal had to deal with a group of stormtroopers. Let BD-1 scan the pattern on the wall.

Treasure #1

This mystery is toward the finish of the way over the reflection point. You can arrive from where you viewed as the past collectible. You'll track down a Priorite Shard.

Star Wars Jedi: Survivor: The Complete Official Guide & Walkthrough

Force Tear #1

You can't get to the mystery during your most memorable visit to Coruscant. The tear is behind the shut entryway where the housetops start, and you should utilize the Lift ability, which you will open progressing in the principal storyline.

Interfacing with the Power Crack starts the test of overcoming 2 Rancors. Attempt to start this battle with an undeniable level person and stay away from supervisor assaults. Likewise assault each Hostility in turn. The prize for finishing the test is 1 Expertise Point.

Renovation Site 4733

List of secrets of Renovation Site 4733

There are 9 collectibles:

- Chest: 2

- Databank: 4

- Treasure: 3

Treasure #1

The secret is in a dark location, which you will reach after completing two wall runs. You'll find a Priorite Shard.

Chest #1

The chest is in a side locked room. BD-1 can open the entryway for you on your most memorable visit to this area.

The chest has a lightsaber grip material.

Databank #1 - Local Directory

The mystery can be tracked down subsequent to passing the instructional exercise on providing orders to a friend in fight. Subsequent to pivoting the enormous bulletin and doing a wall run, you will arrive at an area with a contemplation point and a terminal to filter.

Databank #2 - Desi's Noodles

The collectible is in the location where you encounter the first flying probes. Scan the closed bar.

Treasure #2

The mystery is adjoining where you pass the instructional exercise on utilizing Slow Mode. You need to leap to the bar and afterward to the little rack. You'll track down a Priorite Shard.

Databank #3 - Abandoned Shop

The mystery is located in the lower discretionary region gave the way to the representative's yacht. You arrive not long after opening the alternate way.

Treasure #3

The fortune is located in a dull region under the steps. You can track down it while heading to the congressperson's yacht - not long before the supervisor battle with K-405. You'll track down a Priorite Shard.

Databank #4 - Ascension Cable

This secret is automatically acquired after defeating the K-405 boss. Explore the arena and you will come across the materials to create a climbing rope.

Chest #2

Arriving at the chest can be risky. You need to visit the region where you can run on announcements. Use them to arrive at higher edges and investigate the side region where the chest is.

Industrial Stacks

List of Industrial Stacks secrets

There are 2 collectibles:

- Databank: 2

Databank #1 - Bloody Negotiations

You can find the secret aboard the senator's yacht, after getting inside and interrogating him.

Databank #2 - Stolen Treasures

You need to check the showcase case on board the representative's yacht. You will track down it close to the enormous easy chair.

Undercity Meats

List of Undercity Meats secrets

There are 4 collectibles:

- Chest: 1

- Essence: 2

- Treasure: 1

Chest #1 - Stim Canister

The chest is located close to the reflection point in that area. You need to skip off the upward wall and arrive at the top, then rout the gatekeeper droid.

The chest contains a Stim Canister. This is a vital collectible, since it for all time expands the quantity of BD-1's mending charges by 1.

Essence #1

The mystery is in a dim area, where the game recommends enlightening the region with the lightsaber. You will arrive soon after overcoming the main Cleanse Officer and passing 2 locked entries.

You will acquire a Power update - the Power bar will be for all time broadened.

Essence #2

In the Undercity Meats, you will track down a locked entryway with a blue breaker. You need to hold on until you open BD-1 Electro Dart in the primary storyline. Use it to open the entryway.

You should overcome the smaller than usual manager Excited Jotaz. This will permit you to investigate the room and get the Power redesign - your wellbeing bar will be forever broadened.

Treasure #1

You can get this mysterious solely after you open Merrin's Appeal expertise in the principal storyline permitting you to enter the green doors.

Arrive at the green entryway in the Undercity Meats, enter it, and run the lift. Return rapidly to the passageway for the vacant lift to go up. The mystery is located at the lower part of the deep opening, and it's a Priorite Shard.

Freight Handling Depot

List of Freight Handling Depot secrets

There are 3 collectibles:

- **Chest:** 1
- Essence: 1
- Databank: 1

Databank #1 - Turbo Dogs

The mystery is located in a more modest region behind a room with numerous stormtroopers. Move toward the red garbage can, the one that BD-1 needs to examine. This happens even prior to arriving at the contemplation point.

Chest #1

In the wake of opening the contemplation point, find the region in the image where you can do a long wall run. You will arrive at a rack with the chest - it is over the area with stormtroopers.

The chest has a lightsaber handle material.

Essence #1

You can acquire this mysterious solely after you open Merrin's Appeal expertise in the primary storyline permitting you to enter the green entryways. Start in the primary corridor, snatch a moving compartment, move toward the green door, and play out a scramble in the air.

You will get to another area and in its last part there is a collectible you're searching for.

You will acquire a Power redesign - the Power bar will be forever broadened.

Skylane Regulation Station

List of Skylane Regulation Station secrets

There is 1 collectible:

- Databank: 1

Databank #1 - Gong Droid

When you reach the meditation point in this district, follow the stairs to the lower room. There is an inactive droid that can be scanned by BD-1.

Hangar 2046-C

List of Hangar 2046-C secrets

There are 4 collectibles:

- Chest: 1

- Databank: 1

- Treasure: 2

Databank #1 - Air Traffic Control Perch

You need to run on a couple of hanging boards and arrive at a little region with a gathering of stormtroopers. In the wake of overcoming them, check the wide terminal displayed in the image.

Treasure #1

The mystery can be found in the wake of sliding down the zipline and moving toward the primary piece of the shelter. It is by the railing - you will track down a Priorite Shard.

Treasure #2

Close to Mantis you can experience a Forager Droid. You really want to assault and obliterate him before he get away - smart may be to creep ready and toss a lightsaber. The droid will abandon a Priorite Shard.

Chest #1

Toward the finish of the upper hallway, close to the storage, lies a blue wire. You need to hold on until you open BD-1 Electro Dart in the fundamental storyline. Use it to open the entryway.

You need to overcome a smaller than usual manager D-L1T. This will permit you to examine the gadget and open the new ability to hack DT Guard Droids.

Koboh

Gorge Crash Site

During investigation of Dredger Gorge on planet Koboh in Star Wars Jedi: Survivor, you can commit time to search for collectibles found in the Gorge Crash Site area - the principal zone visited while entering Dredger Gorge. On this page of the aide we show areas of every one of the 14 collectibles from this locale. Finishing these exercises is a compulsory step towards accomplishing 100 percent fruition of Koboh.

List of collectibles in Gorge Crash Site

There are 14 collectiblesto find here:

- Chests: 2

- Essences: 1

- Databanks: 4

- Force Tears: 1

- Treasures: 2

- Seedpods: 4

Seed Pod #1 - Nabooan Green Fire Pineapple

When you leave the lift you took to a level underneath, go to one side of it. There is a plant there that yields Fire Pineapple seeds in the event that you hit it with the lightsaber.

Databank #1 - Broken Dredging Machine

The first databank is generally near the starting point. At the point when you get off the lift, you will see a reflection point before you. Head in the opposite bearing of it, behind the lift from which you've arisen, toward a little bog. There you ought to see a harmed digging machine which you want to examine.

Databank #2 - Broken Mining Droid

Another Databank is right in front from the first. Go to the furthest limit of the marsh - close to a foe there will be a harmed mining droid which you want to examine.

Treasure #1 - Priorite Shard

From the area where found Information base #2, focus on the option to track down a runnable wall. Utilizing it, you can get to a rack which we show in the above screen capture. To arrive, you want to skip off walls until you arrive at it.

When above, search for a home to track down Priorite Shard #1.

Seed Pod #2: Nabooan Green Cactus Ball

Opposite to the lift there is another plant that you can chop down and consequently get seeds. This one is a Desert plant Ball.

Chest #1 - Skrapyard Photoreceptors

Star Wars Jedi: Survivor: The Complete Official Guide & Walkthrough

From the area of Seed Unit #2, return to the reflection point. From that point, search for and climb a rack found practically opposite the lift in which you've shown up. There you'll find a chest containing an appearance thing for BD-1 - Skrapyard Photoreceptors.

Treasure #2 - Priorite Shard

Follow the main accessible street to arrive at a cavern before which there are two B1 Fight Droids. Right at the entry, you can go left where you'll find a wall that can be upward move to arrive at a rack.

Databank #3 - Crushed Prospector

Along the way through the dim passage, you'll experience Databank #3. When you approach the squashed defender, BD-1 will move down and direct the light toward him.

Seed Pod #3 - Cactus Ball

After emerging from the dark cave, opposite you, you'll find another seed pod. In this case, it will be a Cactus Ball once again.

Databank #4 - Koboh Tar

The following collectible (Databank #4) is to some degree further away from the past one. Follow the way and open the easy route to reflection point, use plants to climb and take on a B2 Conflict Droids joined by a rider. When the foes are crushed, you can wall rush to arrive at a rack, and afterward from the line hop down to a stage in a tar lake. Databank #4 is there.

Seed Pod #4 - Fire Pineapple

Just subsequent to finding Databank #4, there is a pit droid in a similar area. Behind it, at the actual edge of the tar lake, there is a tree developing on a slant. Chop it down to get seeds.

Chest #2 - Short Beard

Somewhat further away from the pit droid, on a stone rack among trees and shrubberies (there is likewise a blue covering close by) you'll find Chest #2. Inside, you'll track down an appearance thing - Short Facial hair.

Force Tear #1

When you got Power Ram in your moveset, send the lift found close to the contemplation point up - however let it ride unfilled. You ought to have the option to see a little trapdoor on which you really want to utilize the previously mentioned expertise.

When you're at the lower part of the passage, you'll see the Tear. This preliminary includes overcoming areas of strength for 3 on the double. Finished effectively, the Tear yields a ton of XP.

Essence #1

When you have Power Lift in your moveset, you can lift a submerged boat from the tar lake.

This will uncover the main Quintessence nearby - once gathered, it builds the greatest Power.

Winding Ravine

Whenever you've dominated the capacity to tame wild creatures, you can get to a discretionary, stowed away area. On this page we show areas of all privileged insights from this discretionary district and how to arrive at the entry to it.

How to get to the Winding Ravine?

The entry to the area is located under the Trontoshell. Stand straightforwardly beneath it and press the Manageable button. The huge animal will twist around, and you will actually want to climb it.

At the point when you seize a him, you'll be taken to another zone - Winding Ravine. There are 11 collectibles to view as here.

List of secrets in the Winding Ravine

There are **11** collectiblesto find here:

- Chests: 3

- Essences: 1

Star Wars Jedi: Survivor: The Complete Official Guide & Walkthrough

- Treasures: 2
- Seed Pods: 5

Chest #1 - Warm Material

When you show up to the new region, you can go either left or right. Going left, you'll experience an enormous gathering of rivals and a container that can be utilized as a lift in the space displayed in the screen capture above.

From that point, you can see runnable walls - in one of them, there is a specialty that conceals Warm Material appearance thing.

Essence #1

Wallrunning from the past collectible, you'll arrive at another box that can be utilized as method for pushing the past one. This will get you to the main Quintessence around here. Once gathered, it increments greatest Power.

Chest #2 - Goatee

In the wake of obtaining the Pith, you can put one container on top of the other. This will make an enormous venturing stone to get to the following rack.

Then, bouncing from a wall, you'll arrive at the chest containing Goatee apperance thing.

Treasure #1 - Priorite Shard

Subsequent to gathering the previously mentioned insider facts, you can return to the fork and go right. Hopping between walls inside the cavern you'll at long last arrive at a high rack under the roof - this is where you'll track down Priorite Shard #1.

Treasure #2 - Priorite Shard

In the wake of gathering Shard #1, return the manner in which you came and utilize one of the walls to arrive at a close by passage. It will lead you outside, where you'll see 3 support points - because of them, you can arrive at a rope somewhat further ahead.

At the point when you land, utilize the rope once more and you'll arrive at the highest point of one of the "support points". That is where you'll view as the mystery.

Seed Pods #1-5 - Cactus Ball: Rare

Subsequent to getting the subsequent Fortune, utilize the rope once more and continue forward until you come to the relter. With its assistance, you'll arrive at a stage beneath.

There you'll find 5 plants that can be chopped down to track down seeds. Look out for the foes stationed there.

Chest #3 - Hunter Lightsaber appearance item

Get to the second platform by scaling a chasm and follow the path down. You will reach a chest containing an apperance item.

Water Treatment Works

Treatment Plant - list of secrets

There are 6 collectiblesto find here:

- Chests: 4

- Databanks: 2

Chest #1 - Edgehawk Switch

In the wake of plummeting through the principal hatch, you'll see a few destroyable links. Subsequent to going through them, turn right two times. There are two foes en route, and toward the finish of the way, you'll find a chest containing Edgehawk appearance thing.

Databank #1 - Leaking Water Storage

In the following region, open from the primary seal, you'll experience the first databank of this zone - search for a readable tank toward the side of the room displayed on the guide.

Databank #2 - Lawful Good

In the wake of checking the tank, head higher up and move ahead until you arrive at a carcass and the reverberation.

Chest #2 - Edgehawk Emitter

Assuming you have the scramble capacity as of now, you can turn right and hop over the gorge. Search for the chest there - it contains an apperance thing.

Chest #3 - Edgehawk Grip

Further en route you'll experience a heap of trash which can be eliminated thanks to Supernatural power. Continue forward until you arrive at a chest containing an apperance thing.

Chest #4 - Hairstyle: Scrapper

Look for the door - behind it there is an opponent. At the same location, look for a chest - it will contain a apperance item, namely a new hairstyle.

Corroded Silo

Corroded Silo - list of secrets

There are 6 collectiblesto find here:

- Chests: 3
- Databanks: 3

Databank #1 - Curiosity Sours

Going down you'll experience an entryway on which you really want to utilize Hammer. Behind the entryway, there is a green boundary and a runnable wall. You'll at long last arrive at a readable region toward the end.

Databank #2 - New Acquisitions

Head down until you encounter a Battle Droid. There is a scannable area next to it.

Chest #1 - Goatee and Mustache

In the same location, you'll encounter a chest containing an apperance item.

Chest #2 - Arakyd Heavy

Proceed with the plummet until you arrive at a rope that you can use to get to the other side. In the wake of scaling a wall, you'll see a foe at an edge - kill him. Stand at the foe area and pivot to see a runnable wall.

After a short trip, you'll experience a holder on which you want to utilize Power on.

Chest #3 - Bumpy Rubber

Get back to where the foe was standing and this time head forward and hop from the scaffold to a footbridge underneath.

A little further ahead you'll experience a destroyable boundary behind which there is a holder on which you want to utilize Hammer. The chest contains an apperance thing.

Databank #3 - Whispered Words

Get back to the extremely top and move forward until you experience a little lift that will bring you down. At the base, you'll be gone after by a gathering of rivals. Subsequent to overcoming them, glance the way of the gorge and you'll see a hanging "spoon" on which you can utilize Power. You'll arrive at the other side.

There you'll view as the last, third, databank.

Chamber of Fortitude

How to reach the Chamber of Fortitude?

At the actual lower part of the silo zone there is a gap that can be scaled to arrive at the other side - there is a roundabout entryway there. Open it to uncover a lift. This is the pathway to Chamber of Fortitude. We depict the way in more detail on Chamber of Fortitude page of the Riddles section.

List of secrets in Chamber of Fortitude

There are **5 collectibles**to find here:

- Chests: 1
- Essences: 1
- Databanks: 2
- Treasures: 1

Chest #1 - Two-Tone Metal

Search for the chest in the primary chamber, to one side of the fundamental entry. Open it to track down an apperance thing. Be careful, notwithstanding, of the Anoth Estra supervisor who is viewed as here.

Databank #1 - A World Of Wonder

Not far from the chest you'll find the first databank. Scan it to receive a new entry to the database.

Treasure #1 - Datadisc

The only treasure from this zone is found in the first chamber, to the left not far from the wall.

Databank #2 - Hand In Hand

There is another echo to the right from the entrance to the second chamber.

Essence #1

Search for the Pith in the focal region of the subsequent chamber. Gathering it opens another Advantage - Constancy.

Flooded Bunker

How to get to the Flooded Bunker?

The Flooded Bunker is underneath a little structure located in the focal piece of Drifter's Span. Having Supernatural power will be sufficient to open the entry to the structure, yet to investigate the zone completely, you'll require Lift.

Flooded Bunker - list of secrets

There are 6 collectiblesto find here:

- Chests: 2
- Essences: 1
- Databanks: 2
- Treasures: 1
- Treasure #1 - Priorite Shard

Look for the shard to the right from the entrance. Nevertheless, watch out for a ceiling turret.

Databank #1 - Damage Assessment

You can tear a piece of the front of the bunker with a right power. The new pathway leads down, into a waterway. Figure out how to move out of the water (there are a couple of foes here, so keep an eye out) and you'll track down a readable region.

Chests #1 and #2 - Coated Metal

Subsequent to gathering Databank #1, hop once more into the water and shift focus over to one side - there is a passage there through which you really want to go.

Subsequent to arising on the other side, utilize the plants and afterward use Lift to raise a stage.

On account of it, you can get to the upper floor - when there, shift focus over to one side and you'll see two chests.

Databank #2 - Abandoned Water Filtration System

Get back to the rack from which you've raised the stage with Lift, and you'll see a readable region.

Essence #1

Star Wars Jedi: Survivor: The Complete Official Guide & Walkthrough

From the previous location, go left and you'll reach an essence. It increases your maximum health when collected.

Derelict Dam (Part 1)

As you investigate planet Koboh in Star Wars Jedi: Survivor, you can look for collectibles located in the Derelict Dam, the second area you will visit as you navigate the Dredger Gorge on Koboh. This page of the aide depicts how to track down each of the 47 collectible things. Finishing these exercises is a compulsory step towards accomplishing 100 percent consummation of Koboh.

List of secrets in the Derelict Dam area

There are 47 collectiblesto find here:

- Chests: 8

- Essences: 5

- Databanks: 10

- Force Tears: 1

- Treasures: 10

- Seed Pods: 13.

Databank #1 - Murdered prospector

In the wake of utilizing the winding way driving profound into the derelict dam, you will encounterthree rivals - a B2 fight droid and two ordinary plunderers. Not a long way from the site of the battle with them is Databank #1. It is a killed miner resting under a support point.

Treasure #1 - Priorite Shard

Before you get from the last spot to the contemplation point, from the center piece of the section at the cliff, hop down to the edge beneath. Indeed, even from a higher place, in the wake of turning your back to the reflection point, you will actually want to see the sparkly fortune beneath.

This is another priorite shard.

Chest #1 - Scrapyard body

From the previous location, jump even lower and look to the left. You will find the first chest, which contains a cosmetic item for BD-1 - a scrapyard body.

Databank #2 - Derelict Dam

Descend even lower and head toward the meditation point above. You will be able to scan the destroyed dam - another database.

Seed Pod #1 - Felucian Yellow Cactus Ball

Travel toward the path opposite to the annihilated dam (and the past find). On the shore, close to a gathering of rivals, you will find the seeds of a prickly plant ball.

Databank #3 - Drowned Prospector

On the other bank, only opposite the chest with BD's body part, you will track down the carcass of a miner. In the wake of filtering it, you will get databank #3. Look out for adjacent rivals.

Seed Pod #2 - Felucian Yellow Cactus Ball

While remaining close to the body of the suffocated miner, investigate the right - you will see a save money with the skull of an enormous creature. Close by is another plant with seeds. It will be a cactus ball.

Essence #1

Over the plant from the past subsection you will find a rope that will empower you to get to the wall. With it, you will get to the high edge featured in the above screen capture.

You will find a pith that will provide you with a ton of involvement focuses.

Databank #4 - Gorocco Nest

To one side of the reflection point is a wrecked scaffold. At the point when you go there you will experience a more grounded rival named Gorocco.

Subsequent to overcoming it, you will actually want to bring down the secret entryway located in the wall.

You will wind up in a cave where there is a Gorocco home. Filtering the site will open databank #2.

Essence #2

Being further in the distance, in the previously mentioned depression by the Gorocco home, look to one side. On a slight ascent there is pith #1. In the wake of cooperating with it, your greatest HP will be expanded a little.

Chest #2 - Light Metal

After the gorocco home, return through the imploded scaffold to the reflection site. From that point, go on in the opposite heading to the extension. In the wake of leaping off the slope, go to the edge (you will be gone after by a gathering of foes on the way). There you will find chest #1, which contains the lightsaber material: light metal.

Seed Pod #3 - Felucian Yellow Fire Pineapple

To the right of the chest with light metal, next to the wall to be destroyed, you will find a plant with seeds. In this way you will acquire a fire pineapple.

Bedlam Raider #5 - Dead Bedlam Raider

Get back to the slope from which you as of late bounced (not a long way from the contemplation point) and go on from it. On the way driving down you will track down a dead Commotion Pillager. In the wake of filtering the cadaver, you will open Databank #3.

Seed Pod #4 - Nabooan Green Cactus Ball

Near the dead Bedlam Raider there is a plant. Cut it to get the cactus ball seeds.

Treasure #2 - Priorite Shard

Continue to come across an enemy and a wall to run over. When you find yourself on the other side, you will come across treasure #1 lying next to a large stone - this will be another priorite shard.

Databank #6 - Dam flow pipes

Close to the box of light metal is a construction covered with a wall to be obliterated. Bounce on the construction being referred to and go to the lines apparent among the shrubs. In the wake of checking them you will open databank #6.

Databank #7 - Disintegrating dam wall

Next go to one side, then stand on the metal component suspended over the pool of tar. Subsequent to checking the wall opposite you will open databank #7.

Chest #3 - Hairstyle: mullet

At the point when you move higher by hopping between the stages on the tar lake and afterward rout the two rivals, you will see another tar lake with stages. Use them to get to the little island.

There you will find a chest that contains a haircut for Cal - mullet.

Databank #8 - Desperate Escape

A piece farther from the lake with tar, you will witness a little occasion including rivals. Hop down there and head further into the cavern. To one side of the entry you will track down a thing to check. In this manner you will open the #8 databank.

Chest #4 - Anodized metal

After defeating the first BX Droid, you will be able to go through the tunnel to the right. Inside the room you will see a wall that will allow you to get to a higher shelf.

There is a chest hiding anodized metal for personalizing materials.

Treasure #3 - Priorite Shard

Opposite the chest with anodized metal, in the corner of the room near the door, you will find another priorite shard.

Chest #5 - Jacket: tactical

You will get to the fifth chest by going directly from where you battled the primary BX Droid. Subsequent to hopping into through the opening, you will confront a foe and a chest located close by. It conceals a strategic coat.

Derelict Dam (Part 2)

The second area you will visit while crossing the Dredger Gorge on Koboh in Star Wars Jedi Survivor is the Derelict Dam. In our aide you will track down the areas of every one of the 47 collectibles. This will make it more straightforward for you to investigate the planet Koboh at 100%.

List of secrets in the Derelict Dam area

There are 47 collectiblesto find here:

- Chests: 8

- Essences: 5

- Databanks: 10

- Force Tears: 1

- Treasures: 10

- Seed Pods: 13

Treasure #4 - Priorite Shard

Since you gain the capacity to fake mines, you will actually want to visit a few additional spots. In the wake of annihilating the dam, the level of the tar lake that you recently used to get the mullet hairdo will even out. Return there and you will see another nook that you can enter.

There you will track down another Priorite shard.

Treasure #5 - Priorite shard

Another shard is located on a newly exposed islet, which you can jump onto - on the way to the chest with the mullet hairstyle. Another Priorite shard is located there.

Databank #9 - Bones of the creature

You can likewise bait a mine to the area with the workbench. From the slant close by you can see the wall to be obliterated.

Then you really want to stroll through the passage as far as possible. En route you will be gone after by a few rivals, including Gorocco. At the end you will view as a fossil. Check it to open Databank #9.

Treasure #6 - Priorite shard

By the fossil from the past subsection , there is a rope that you can use to get to the top. While nearby the rope, glance around while peering down. You will see the stones where another fortune is located.

It will be another Priorite Shard.

Databank #10 - Abandoned camp

After picking up the previous collectible, return to the top and walk ahead. You will be attacked by two droids and mines. Then you will find the next item to scan. This will be databank #10.

Seed Pod #5 - Cactus ball

Almost exactly in the same place as in the previous subsection is a plant. Cutting it down will give you cactus ball seeds.

Essence #3

A piece further on, between the entryway and the huge lift, you will find a spot with a pith that expands how much greatest Power.

Seed Pod #6 - Fire pineapple

After the scene involving the great Trontoshell, you will find a plant from which you can get the fire pineapple seeds.

Chest #6 - Scrapyard Head

After using the elevator, you will find yourself in an area with a rather large group of opponents. After the fight, take care of placing the block against the wall so you can jump on it and get to the ledge.

You will find a crate that contains a cosmetic item for BD-1 - a scrapyard head.

Chest #7 - Two-tone metal

You will actually want to open the seventh carton solely after finishing the fifth section, in which you will acquire the capacity to utilize BD-1's electro darts.

The chest is where the entryway is, behind which is Vashtan Wolfe. Shoot the wire, then rapidly open the chest. Subsequent to securing its items, you should take on a manager conflict.

Chest #8 - Increasing the stim limit

You can utilize the lift close to the workbench (on the slope) to get higher up, where there is a door that you can open with the lift expertise.

Behind the door there is an entry by which you will reach the point where the incredible rival, Gorocco Matron, dwells. Subsequent to killing it, you will actually want to purge the carton located close by - this way you will build the constraint of stims you have.

Seed Pods #7, #8 and #9

From a similar spot where you battled Gorocco Matron, you can see expands that will get you to the level above.

When you are at the top head to one side. You will see three plants in a single spot. Among them you will track down the seeds of the intriguing fire pineapple.

Treasure #7 - Priorite shard

To the left of the aforementioned seeds you will find another Priorite shard.

Essence #4

Across from the last collectible, you will find an essence that will give you a great deal of experience.

Derelict Dam (Part 3)

Star Wars Jedi: Survivor: The Complete Official Guide & Walkthrough

List of secrets in the Derelict Dam area

There are 47 collectiblesto find here:

- Chests: 8
- Essences: 5
- Databanks: 10
- Force Tears: 1
- Treasures: 10
- Seed Pods: 13.

Seed Pod #10 - Fire pineapple: alderaan blue

Not a long way from where the depicted region closes, there is a kind of lift where you can utilize the Hammer expertise. This will permit you to get to a higher edge.

From that point, go to one side and to the furthest limit of the way - you will end up at a tree that will give you more seeds.

Essence #5

Going further you will experience a few rivals. Then again, on the roof where the three droids are remaining, there is a gadget that you can use to obliterate the congested entry. The circle you really want for this is to one side of the entry being referred to.

In the following room, subsequent to involving BD-1 for hacking, you will find a mine that you should manual for a wall that can be obliterated.

Then you are left with utilizing BD-1 to consume off the development and bounce over the walls. When you are at the top, utilize the main accessible way - toward the finish of it you will find an embodiment that will give you another advantage space.

Treasure #8 - Priorite Shard

Where you found the circle used to take out the Koboh matter, there are walls that you can hop on to the edge above. There is another priorite shard.

Databank - Dredger Gorge Raid

On the platform where chest #3 was previously located is another databank entry.

Treasure #9 - Priorite Shard

At the point when you arrive at the reflection point located at the earliest reference point of the Southern Arrive at region, you might see a wall that can be hopped up to a higher edge.

There is another priote shard located there.

Force Tear #1 - Fractured Agility

To get to the last piece of the collectibles, you should initially free the enormous bird in the Forest Array. Then head to the Bubbling Feign region and get to the bird being referred to.

It will be important to get to a higher edge, which you will just do with the assistance of creatures meandering around.

Then with the utilization of inflatables you will ultimately get to the bird, on which you should utilize the expertise that permits you to tame creatures.

In this manner you will return to the Derelict Dam - essentially a locale of it that you were unable to visit previously. Opposite the arrival region is a Power Tear, where you will be entrusted with handling a deftness challenge.

Seed Pod #11 - Fire Pineapple

Across from the Force Tear you will find another seed, this time a Fire Pineapple.

Seed Pod #12 - Fire Pineapple

From the last seed go slightly to the right - you will find another portion of seeds.

Seed Pod #13 - Fire Pineapple

The last seeds to be found in this area are to the right of the elevator.

Treasure #10 - Priorite Shard

To one side of the previously mentioned lift, yet marginally lower you can see a Forager Droid. Kill it (we portrayed how t o do it on the page How to get a scavengere droid?), and you will triumph when it's all said and done the last fortune. Assuming you miss it, you can reset the world at the contemplation point and attempt once more.

Southern Reach (Part 1)

The Southern Reach is important for the bigger Drifter's Reach area in the world Kobohin Star Wars Jedi Survivor. This page of the aide portrays how to track down every one of the 33 collectible things. This will be one of the moves toward investigate the planet Koboh at 100%.

List of secrets in the Southern Reach area

There are 33 collectiblesto find here:

- Chests: 3

- Essences: 1

- Databanks: 3

- Treasures: 7

- Seed Pods: 19

Seed Pod #1 - Bluebell Squish: nabooan green

After the cutscene, you will come across a small tree while going down the path. Cutting it down will give you Bluebell Squish seeds.

Chest #1 - Full Beard

Jump onto the shelf located behind Mosey's post. There is chest #1 containing the cosmetic item Full Beard.

Seed Pod #2 - Tuber Maw: nabooan green

Subsequent to exhausting the previously mentioned chest, go to the clearing precisely opposite. You will go over a little gathering of gorgers. Close by, nonetheless, there is a plant with which you will get Tuber Throat seeds.

Treasure #1 - Priorite Shard

From the place where you obtained the seeds from the previous subsection, you may notice a ledge.

After climbing it, look for a nest where there is another priorite shard.

Chest #2 - Kashyyk Paints

Close to the home, where the past find was, there are poles, so you can get to the other side. You will experience plants impeding the doorways to the cavern.

Behind the plants is a little cavern, where you will be gone after by two Bramliks. Subsequent to disposing of them, utilize the following bar to bounce further. Subsequent to pivoting, you will see another little cavern.

In a chest remaining in a cavern is a corrective thing of Kashyyyk Paints.

Databank #1 - Enchanted

From the spot where you viewed as the last collectible, you can go to one side and bounce down to the edge beneath (you can likewise arrive at similar spot from the plants referenced in the past subsection). There you will see a rope that will permit you to get to the slope on the opposite side.

There you will track down a spot to examine - this way you will open databank #1.

Essence #1

To the left of the previous find is another one - this time it is an essence that will give you a great deal of experience.

Seed Pod #3 - Tuber Maw: Felucian yellow

Get back to the recently referenced rope - at the base is Gorocco, in the wake of overcoming which you will get a great deal of involvement focuses. Not a long way from where he was, you can track down another seed.

Treasure #2 - Datadisk

From the spot where you battled Gorocco, go down the passage apparent close by and , making a beeline for the right, get out.

You will run over a gathering of battling monsters. In the wake of managing them, go to a close by structure, where you will hear an uncommon sound. There you will see a scrounger droid, subsequent to killing which you will get an information plate.

Databank #2 - Unusual silo

Slightly to the left of the previous find is a place to scan - this is databank #2.

Seed Pod #4 - Cactus ball: alderaan blue

You can get to this plant by following the path down from where the Mosey's stand is. Along the way you will find cactus seeds, right next to a rock wall.

Seed Pod #5 - Tuber Maw

You will reach a structure, opposite of which there is a little tree - in the wake of obliterating it you will get Tuber Throat seeds.

Databank #3 - Amphibian blues

Over the precipice located precisely opposite the recently discharged chest (with kashyyyk paints), you will find another databank section. On the off chance that it's not currently here, you want to advance in the story somewhat further.

Southern Reach (Part 2)

While investigating the Drifter's Reach in the world Koboh in Star Wars Jedi: Survivor, you can look for collectibles located in the Southern Reach - the principal area you will visit while crossing the Drifter's Reach in the world Koboh. This page of the aide portrays how to track down every one of the 33 collectible things. This will be one of the moves toward investigate the planet Koboh at 100%.

List of secrets in the Southern Reach area

There are **33 collectibles** to find here:

- Chests: 3
- Essences: 1
- Databanks: 3
- Treasures: 7
- Seed Pods: 19

Seed Pod #6, #7, #8 and #9 - Tuber Maw: rare

In the event that you have proactively opened the capacity to tame creatures, you can utilize the assistance of a little flying animal that will assume you to the position showed in the above screen capture. The said animal is near the starting point around here.

Subsequent to landing, you will discover a few trees from which you will get seeds.

Some of them are a little lower, yet at the same time nearby the others.

Seed Pod #10 and #11 - Tuber Maw

Close to where the past ones were found - simply go a little in reverse from that point.

By the stones and close to the edge is another part of seeds.

Seed Pod #12 - Tuber Maw

Still within the same area, you will find more Tuber Maw seeds.

Seed Pod #13 - Tuber Maw

Another portion of the seeds is a little further away from the others. This is the last one you will find on this hill.

Treasure #3 - Priorite Shard

In a small alcove nearby you will find another priorite shard.

Treasure #4 - Priorite Shard

From the spot where you gathered a ton of seeds prior, you can go a little lower, to the top of the silo. At the actual edge of it you will find another priorite shard.

Seed Pod #14 - Spine Fluff: rare

Yet again to get to the seeds of another sort, you should utilize the assistance of a flying animal close to the start of the area. You can utilize it to get to the slopes set apart in the screen capture above.

There you will find intriguing Spine Cushion seeds.

Treasure #5 - Priorite shard

Right next to where the flying creature is, you will find another priorite shard.

Seed Pod #15 - Spine Fluff: alderaan blue

Under the hill where you found the previous collectibles and by the river, there are more seeds - this time Spine Fluff: Alderaan blue.

Seed Pod #16 - Spine Fluff

Nearby, in front of the dam itself, there is another plant from which you will take seeds - another Spine Fluff.

Treasure #6 - Priorite shard

A similar dam at which you found the above seeds can be opened with the Power Lift. This way you will get to the following priorite shard.

Treasure #7 - Priorite shard

A corpse skull hangs at the entrance to the Rambler's Reach Outpost. Take it down with the Force Pull, and you will get another priority shard.

Chest #3 - Quickdraw

Getting to the last chest in this space is very muddled. The structure concealing it is located close to the entry to the Drifter's Reach Station. At the point when you obliterate the entryway prompting the inside, there will be Koboh matter in your method for annihilating.

To dispose of it, you should go to the adjoining region (Tracker's Quarry) to open the entry to the cavern utilizing Power Lift.

Inside, you should find the circle, which is located somewhere down in the cavern - en route to it, keep as high as conceivable to stay away from death.

Subsequent to getting the circle, toss it to the comparing intensifier, and the laser bar will open another section to ultimately raise a ruckus around town you need to get to.

From that point, utilize the BD-1's Koboh processor and obliterate the matter impeding the entry. Inside you will track down a chest with a restorative things for your blaster.

Seed Pod #17 - Spine Fluff: alderaan blue

If you already have unlocked the dash skill, use the grappling hook rope over Gorocco to get to the hill shown in the screenshot above. You can find Tuber Maw seeds there.

Seed Pod #18 - Tuber Maw

From the above-mentioned place you can get lower - to the ledge below the place where you got the Essence earlier. There you will find more Tuber Maw seeds.

Seed Pod #19 - Tuber Maw

The last seed pod is in a cave near Gorocco, over which there is a rope.

Hunter's Quarry

Star Wars Jedi: Survivor: The Complete Official Guide & Walkthrough

During the investigation of Drifter's Reach Station on planet Koboh in Star Wars Jedi: Survivor, you can go over an entry to Hunter's Quarry, an enormous separate locale. On this page of our aide, we supply a rundown and careful areas of each of the 23 mysteries tracked down in this zone among them chests, treasures, or databanks.

List of secrets in Hunter's Quarry

There are 23 collectiblesto find here:

- Chests: 3
- Essences: 2
- Databanks: 9
- Force Tears: 1
- Treasures: 2
- Seed Pods: 6

Seed Pod #1 - Cactus ball

From the entry to the area, continue into the heading of a little slope in the western piece of the district. The Seed Unit is at the slope's edge.

Seed Pod #2 - Cactus ball

Another Seed Pod can be found opposite to the previous collectible.

Databank #1 - The Wise Hunters

Continue going west and follow the path leading up.

You'll reach a cave inside of which there is another scannable area - after passing through the fissure, turn left.

Chest #1 - Bomber's Jacket

Standing at the Databank #1 location, turn right and proceed to the end - there you'll find a chest containing an appearance item.

Databank #2 - A New Beginning

Leave the cavern and continue north-west through the base region. You'll track down a camp - at its entry there is a reverberation to check. Remember and look out for rivals in the actual camp.

Chest #2 - Light Metal

From the Databank #2 location, turn right and look for the chest at a burning gate.

Databank #3 - A Task Too Far

To the right of Chest #2 you'll find a corpse that can be scanned.

Databank #4 - A Mechanical Touch

From the area of Databank #2, circumvent the close by building and do a wall run then utilize the plants. You'll wind up in a space from which you can get to the inside of the structure. Following hopping down you will track down an area to examine.

Databank #5 - A Gift Revoked

Look for Databank #5 opposite from the previous collectible.

Treasure #1 - Priorite Shard

Look for the priorite shard at the same location.

Essence #1

Close by in the room there is a gadget through which you can bring a Mine Droid. Use it to open the exit from the structure, in particular obliterate the entryway.

Outside, straightforwardly directly from the leave, there is another way to annihilate.

Behind them you'll track down an Embodiment that expands the greatest measure of Power.

Seed Pod #3 - Pine Fern

Return to the location entrance, but this time go east. You'll find seed pods.

Databank #6 - The Koboh Emergence

For the following collectible, you want to get inside the cavern from which you've carried the laser to annihilate the development in one of the structures of Drifter's Reach. The quickest way includes reaching the region from which the laser bar arises.

When there, eliminate the ball from the gadget and hush up about it close, go into a little room on the right.

Place it in the following gadget and you'll have the option to examine the region.

Essence #2

The following substance (granting a great deal of XP) isn't a long way from the area of Databank #6. Taking the ball with you won't assist with this one, so get to the collectible area straightaway and associate with it.

Databank #7 - An Honest Appraisal

Convey the ball back to the laser gadget. Presently go as would the laser pillar fire - back outside.

Rather than leaving, hop down and go into a room on the left - you'll track down a platform for the ball there-use it.

This opens another Databank.

Treasure #2 - Datadisk

From the area of Databank #7, go to the close by exit. Keep to the left side and before long you'll experience plants that you can climb.

At the top, continue toward the bird roosted on a bluff. Close to the bird, there is an inflatable - use it to sling yourself to next ones.

At last, reach a runnable wall - it will lead you to a little concealing spot in the stones. Plunder the chest.

Force Tear - Fractured Delusion

In the same place you'll find a Force Tear - the related challenge involves fighting a group of opponents.

Seed Pod #4 - Pine Fern

From the location of the Force Tear, once again use the baloons to reach an opposite hill (the one with large bones). Seed Pod #4 is there.

Seed Pod #5 - Pine Fern

The next Seed Pod is exactly opposite the previous one, at the other end.

Seed Pod #6 - Pine Fern

From the location of Seed Pod #5, turn right and reach the nearest bones.

Chest #3 - Hunter Jacket

Return to the large skull and carefully jump down. The chest with the appearance item is there. Watch out for the nearby Goroko.

Databank #8 - Gorocco Sanctuary

Look for a nearby column - a database entry can be found there.

Databank #9 - Free Sample

Staying close to the edge, proceed right to the end of the path. You'll find another databank there.

Pyloon's Saloon

The Pyloon's Saloon is another area accessible straightforwardly from Drifter's Reach Outpost settlement on planet Koboh in Star Wars Jedi Survivor. On this page of our aide, you can find a list and definite locations of each of the 5 secrets that can be tracked down in this small structure.

Pyloon's Saloon - list of secrets

There are 5 collectibles to find here:

- Chests: 2

- Databanks: 2
- Treasures: 1

Chest #1 - Scrapper Outfit

The chest with the appearance item is in the room where you can rest.

Databank #1 - Hallikset

The echo is in the same room, right from Chest #1. It hangs on the wall.

Treasure #1 - Priorite Shard

This is the main Treasure in this zone - to get it, you want to get on the upper level of the bar, and afterward visit a small room left from the fundamental stairs. Go on by cooperating with the latrine. The activity is compensated with an accomplishment Tidying Up.

Chest #2 - Eerin Siinaa Music Track

To reach the last collectible region, you really want to keep conversing with Moran until the entryway behind him opens. Sadly, after every conversation, you want to go outside the saloon.

With enough conversations, you'll get access to the previously mentioned room. Inside, there is a chest containing another music track.

Databank #2 - Moran's Possessions

Exactly opposite Chest #2, there is a scannable area.

Sodden Grotto

Sodden Grotto is another area accessible from Drifter's Reach Outpost on Koboh. On this page of our Star Wars Jedi Survivor guide, you can find a list and locations of each of the 8 secrets showing up around here among them chests, treasures, or databanks.

Sodden Grotto - list of secrets

There are 8 collectiblesto find here:

- Chests: 1
- Essences: 1
- Databanks: 4
- Treasures: 2

Treasure #1 - Priorite Shard

Right toward the start of the area, you want to destroy a wall impeding the way ahead. When the way is clear, follow the way down to its furthest limit. There you'll track down the shard.

Databank #1 - Dead Researcher

Get back to the entry and destroy another obstacle. Proceed until you reach a chasm and an opening in the wall behind it. Hop into the opening to find another databank.

Databank #2 - Dead Gorgers

Head back, go through the chasm, and make the way of cables. There will be more ahead. Behind the cables, turn right and go on until you reach a couple of Dead Gorgers. Scan one of them to get the collectible.

Treasure #2 - Priorite Shard

Behind the dead Gorgers there is a gap that you can go through. Inside, you'll find a burrowing droid which is your target.

Chest #1 - BD-1 - Scrapyard Legs

Follow the dull street almost straightforwardly straight from the previously mentioned hole. Follow the way until you experience the chest, which contains an apperance thing for BD-1. Keep an eye out for two opponents nearby.

Databank #3 - Massive Ribcage

Return to the region where the tunneling droid was before and continue toward the lit passage where water falls from a higher place. Soon, you'll experience another hole. It will prompt a stage where you really want to go left - you'll reach huge bones that must be scanned.

Databank #4 - Prospector Remains

Continue forward and turn left at the first opportunity. You'll find another echo.

Essence #1

Move ahead and hop down to an enormous square. You can see the essence from the upper floor. Be careful, nonetheless, of a boss that might hide on the square. This Essence grants another Advantage.

Riverbed Watch

During investigation of Drifter's Reach Outpost on planet Koboh in Star Wars Jedi: Survivor, you can run over a district called Riverbed Watch. On this page, you can find a list and locations of every one of the 12 secrets that show up there among them chests, treasures, or databanks.

List of secrets in Riverbed Watch

There are 12 collectibles to find here:

- Chests: 1

- Essences: 1

- Databanks: 4

- Treasures: 2

- Seed Pods: 4

Databank #1 - Doma, Unbowed

From the region entrance, travel to its north-western corner - you'll encounter a corpse there. Scan it to unlock Databank #1.

Seed Pod #1 - Spine Fluff

Proceed in the direction of the river - you'll find the seed pod at the river bank.

Seedbags #2 and #3 - Spine Fluff

Look for #2 and #3 on the other side of the river.

Seed Pod #4 - Tuber Maw

From the locations of #2 and #3, proceed in the direction of Corroded Silo region. Look for the seed pod at the silo wall.

Treasure #1 - Priorite Shard

Follow the river until you reach a small islet - there you'l find a burrowing droid.

Databank #2 - Battle Droid Blues

Not a long way from the tunneling droid, there is a cavern that the droid uses as his escape course. Inside you'll find another databank.

Databank #3 - The Warlord's Standard

Go to the area of the entry to Corroded Silo - there you'll find a runnable wall and a rope that you can use to access the close by reflection point.

The scannable region is not a long way from it.

Databank #4 - A Brokered Alliance

When inside the structure, you can scale by skipping from one wall to another. Go on by climbing the net. At the top, you'll need to confront a huge gathering of various Fight Droids. When the danger is dealt with, search for the reverberation, which is close by.

Treasure #2 - Priorite Shard

Enter the building and go straight. You should find another Priorite Shard.

Chest #1 - Hairstyle - Bun

You need to climb even higher using structures ahead. At the edge of the canopy you'll find the chest containing the hairstyle.

Essence #1

Look for the essence right from Chest #1 - it increases maximum health.

Foothilll Falls

Lower region Falls is a zone from planet Koboh of Star Wars Jedi: Survivor. It is a piece of Prospector's Imprudence bigger district. On this page of our aide, we supply a list and show locations of each of the 12 collectibles you can arrive among them chests, treasures, or databanks.

Foothill Falls - list of secrets

There are 12 collectiblesto find here:

- Chests: 4

- Databanks: 4

- Treasures: 2

- Seed Pods: 2

Chest #1 - Hairstyle - Slicked Back

Use the line saw as close to Prospector to reach the other side. Following landing, circle the small structure on the right. The chest (containing another hairstyle) is there.

Databank #1 - Cargo Elevator

Across from the previously mentioned constructing (or where you've come from), there is a freight lift that can be scanned.

Databank #2 - A Curious Pair

Look for the databank near the flying creature found nearby.

Treasure #1 - Priorite Shard

From the databank #2 location run straight for the lone rock. Look for the Priorite in bushes near the wall and edge.

Chest #2 - Pommel: Patience

At the Treasure #1 area, find where you can hop into water. The chest (containing an appearance thing) is on the lower part of the tank.

Seed Pod #1 - Koboh Spiker: Nabooan Green

Get back to the area with the flying animal and use it to fly over the chasm. The seed case is in that general area, at the edge of the shelf.

Seed Pod #2 - Koboh Spiker

From the previous area, head towards the structure where there is a gathering of commotion riders. The seeds are close by.

Databank #3 - Child's Hideaway

Go back to the shelf where you've collected Seed Pod #1. From there, head right. You should come across the databank.

Treasure #2 - Priorite Shard

Not far from Databank #3, there is a Nekko close to a wall - use him to reach the shelf above the previous collectible.

Databank #4 - Prospecting Network

Mount a Nekko and return to the aforementioned building. In its vicinity there is a runnable wall - this way you can access the upper floor.

A balloon is there, which allows you to climb even higher.

The scannable structure is at the end of the path.

Chest #3 - Droid Paint

Straightforwardly opposite the previous collectible there is a chest containing an appearance thing. Gaining admittance to it requires Power Lift and Power Slam.

Chest #4 - Stim upgrade

Getting to the last collectible is more muddled. First you need to leap to the shelf underneath - there you'll find a mine droid dispenser.

Bring the mine droid to a structure underneath and destroy the entryway by accessing it through an opening in the roof.

Everything is passed on to do is plunder the chest - it increases the quantity of conveyed Stims.

Smuggler's Tunnels

Smuggler's Tunnels in the world Koboh is partitioned into several parts, one of which is Smuggler's Tunnels. On this page of the manual for Star Wars Jedi Survivor, you will find descriptions of each of the 13 secrets that can be gathered there - including chests, treasures, or databanks.

How to get to the Smuggler's Tunnels?

You will get to the Smuggler's Tunnels from the hideaway in the Pyloon Saloon - the entry is taken cover behind a household item. Notwithstanding, to gather every one of the secrets, it is smarter to enter this region from another area set apart in the screenshots above - one of the buildings in Drifter's Reach Outpost. For this you really want a mount, which will assist you with getting inside the structure.

Some of the secrets must be accessed subsequent to finishing the last chapters of the game - the last capacity required for them is opened in the course of the fifth section of the game.

List of secrets in the Smuggler's Tunnels

There are 13 collectiblesto find here:

- Chests: 1

- Essences: 2

- Databanks: 5

- Force Tears: 1

- Treasures: 2

Databank #1 - List of Grievances

Once inside, you will find an object to scan on one of the tables.

Treasure #1 - Priorite Shard

To the right of the green barrier lies a Priorite Shard.

Treasure #2 - Priorite Shard

Get through the green barrier and jump down. At the fork of the dark tunnel, turn left - there is a Priorite Shard at the end of the path.

Databank #2 - Jailbreak Inventory

Keep strolling the main way until you reach a lit room. In the wake of scanning the garbage on the left you will find another databank section.

Treasure #3 - Priorite Shard

To the right of the last collectible against the wall is another Priorite shard.

Databank #3 - Death in the Dark

After picking up the previous collectible, squeeze through the gap. You will get out next to a corpse, from which you will collect another entry in the databank.

Databank #4 - One Last Victory

In the wake of getting the last collectible, hop into the hall located to one side of the green obstruction by the wall. There you will track down a corpse to scan.

Treasure #4 - Priorite Shard

Next to the corpse is a jug. After destroying it, you will get a Priority Shard.

Essence #1

En route to the following secret, you must play out some acrobatics - get past a series of green barriers and do a wall run. Toward the finish of the manner in which you will find an Essence that will give you another advantage slot.

Force Tear #1 - Fractured Momentum

Star Wars Jedi: Survivor: The Complete Official Guide & Walkthrough

In the wake of opening the closed entryway, head left and use the bar to get to the other side. From that point, set out toward the hindrance which will become visible somewhat further on. Behind it is the Power Tear with an arcade challenge.

Chest #1 - Bottoms: tactical

Return from the area of the last collectible and hop into the water. At the base you will track down a chest with a cosmetic thing. You will find the chest almost straightforwardly under the entryway you've as of late opened.

Essence #2

Return to the entryway opened previously and reach the region with a green boundary and some garbage. There, head left and hop down. Subsequent to overcoming a gathering of opponents, find the Essence located close to the wall. Essence will provide you with a lot of involvement points.

Databank #5 - No Way Out

After collecting the Essence, keep moving forward. Squeeze through a narrow gap and head left.

Collapsed Passage

Collapsed Passage is a small area in whuch you can see as just a single collectible. On this page of the Star Wars Jedi Survivor guide, we've described how to arrive and gather the Datadisc.

How to reach the Collapsed Passage?

You will get to the Collapsed Passage as you advance in the story. To restore there, use the Reflection Point or the vines close to the Power Tear in the Smuggler's Tunnels. The spot is shown in the screens above.

List of secrets in the Collapsed Passage location

There is 1 collectible:

- Treasure: 1

Treasure - Datadisc

From the Reflection Point, push ahead, bouncing on platforms and from one wall to another. At last you will get to the Chamber of Duality. From that point, hop down to a small stage.

There you will find a Datadisc.

Chamber of Duality

On this page of the manual for Star Wars Jed: Survivor, you will track down a description of every one of the 4 secrets in the Chamber of Duality area. We've listed every one of the treasures, chests, and databanks in this piece of Drifter's Reach.

How to get to the Chamber of Duality?

You will get to the Chamber of Duality from the Collapsed Passage. Notwithstanding, if you need to return there after some time, you can use a lift in Drifter's Reach Outpost. The specific area is shown in the image above.

List of secrets in the Chamber of Duality

There are 4 collectiblesto find here:

- Chests: 1
- Essences: 1
- Databanks: 1
- Treasures: 1

Databank #1 - Disaster

Before you go through the gap to the central part of the chamber, you can scan the structure you've passed before.

Essence #1

Across from the gap through which you entered the main part of the chamber, you will find Essence - after interacting with it, you will get a new perk.

Chest #1 - Jedi Paint

In the event that you focus on the left from the essence referenced above, you might see a chest on an edge a little further down. You can arrive by wall running. In the chest you will track down a cosmetic thing.

Treasure #1 - Datadisc

To have the option to get the last collectible, you must solve the riddle first, which is necessary to solve the issue in the storyline. When you get to the new opening in the wall, you will find a datadisc.

Phon'Qi Caverns (Part 1)

Phon'Qi Caverns is a district in the world Koboh in Star Wars: Jedi Survivor. On this page of the aide you will find the locations of every one of the 31 secrets that can be gathered in this piece of the Drifter's Reach, including chests, treasures or databanks.

How to get to Phon'Qi Caverns?

You will get to the Phon'Qi Caverns from the spot demonstrated in the screenshots over: the basement in the structure located in Foothills Falls. To open the portal, you will require the Lift skill. More data on this can be tracked down in the Puzzles and Reaching Phon'Qi Caverns chapters.

Some of the secrets must be accessed in the wake of finishing the last chapters of the game - the last skill required for them is opened in the course of the fifth part of the game.

List of secrets in Phon'Qi Caverns

There are 31 collectibles to find here:

- Chests: 7

- Essences: 3

- Databanks: 14

- Treasures: 7

Databank #1 - Makeshift Grave

As soon as you get into the basement of the aforementioned building, you will find a corpse from which you can sense an echo.

Databank #2 - Abandoned Corpse

Proceeding, you will go over a hole hindered with metal sheets - eliminate it with the Lift skill. In the wake of passing through it, go directly ahead (toward the right you'll have a reflection point). You'll track down another reverberation.

Databank #3 - Cavern Fungus

Then go directly ahead and lift the structure covering the opening. Hop down to it and quickly run and hop forward - several bridges will collapse. From that point onward, you will have the potential chance to scan the spot and gain another section.

Essence #1

Use a snare to get to the wall above you, then leap to the one on the left - you will get to a high edge. From that point, run along the wall to the following edge and you will see the essence before you. You will get a great deal of involvement from this.

Databank #4 - Cave Turbolift Caverns

Turn towards the walls you just used and get one of the bombs developing on it. Toss it at the hindrance on the passage a piece further away.

Use the new passage. You will be gone after by a boss named Sebb Eshan.

In the wake of overcoming him, you will get a ton of XP. You can also scan close by doors.

Chest #1 - Emitter: Duelist

In the wake of getting the previous collectible, turn upward and you'll see a stone block that you can drop using the Slam skill.

You will open a passage to the base - there is a chest with a cosmetic component.

Databank #5 - A Gen'Dai Plots

Get back to the top and pursue another faster route back to where you scanned the Sinkhole Fungus. From that point, follow the way, which you have not yet visited, further into the cavern. You will be gone after by a gathering of enemies. You will find another databank section by one of the walls.

Databank #6 - Raider Depot

Jump down through the nearby hole and scan the computer. You will receive another databank entry. Watch out for the cannon near the ceiling.

Chest #2 - Material: Bomber

Stay at the bottom and go forward. Along the way, you will encounter two more cannons. At the end of the path, you will find a chest with a cosmetic element.

Databank #7 - Rancor Prey

Return upstairs and locate the stone under the roof (across from the pit that you've just escaped) - drop it with a Slam and it will open a passage to the base. Then leap to the extremely base, where you will confront an incredible foe. Subsequent to overcoming him, you will actually want to scan the skeletons in his sanctuary.

Treasure #2 - Datadisc

Near the previous collectible, there is a datadisc.

Databank #8 - A Cave Too Far

While still at the bottom, head deeper into the cave. You'll come across the next databank entry.

Databank #9 - As Above, As Below

Close by you will find a bomb, which you can use to destroy the obstruction close by.

Another boss will rise up out of the new passage. There is another databank section in the room where the boss was.

Chest #3 - Activator: Duelist

In the location where you picked up the previous collectible, use the hook to get to the top. You will find a chest with a cosmetic element.

Chest #4 - Pommel: Duelist

Return downstairs and to the spot where you took the bomb (to one side of the room exit). There, bounce endlessly lower. Going ahead, watch out for the overwhelming majority detonating enemies that will come your direction. You will reach water. There will be a chest at the base.

Treasure #3 - Datadisc

Return to the surface and use the close by wall to get back to the top - when you move higher, there will be another wall before you. You will get to a passage with many jugs. Go to the small cavern on the left - there is a datadisc in one of the jugs. Watch out for the adversary located there.

Treasure #4 - Datadisc

Go to one side of the spot where you viewed as the previous collectible; you will get back to the fundamental lobby. There are two enemies there (albeit one of them further away and probably won't go after you). There is also another treasure in one of the jugs.

Treasure #5 - Datadisc

In one of the jugs next to the blocked passage, you will find another datadisc.

Treasure #6 - Datadisc

Starting at the location of the previous collectible, go to a small cave near the gate - there is an elevator. You will find another datadisc in one of the jugs at the edge over the precipice.

Phon'Qi Caverns (Part 2)

In Star Wars Jedi: Survivor, you can go to the Phon'Qi Caverns in Rambler's Reach on the planet Koboh. Our guide will help you find all 31 secrets from that region, including chests, treasures and databanks.

List of secrets in Phon'Qi Caverns

Star Wars Jedi: Survivor: The Complete Official Guide & Walkthrough

There are 31 collectibles to find here:

- Chests: 7

- Essences: 3

- Databanks: 14

- Treasures: 7

Databank #10 - Scientific Frisson

Use the lift and you will get to a more elevated level and return to where you have proactively been (thus opening a shortcut). Get one of the bombs to destroy the previously referenced door. From that point onward, a boss battle awaits you. There, you will also find a databank section.

Chest #5 - Grip: Duelist

Head down to reach the green barrier. Behind it, there will be a chest containing a cosmetic weapon item.

Essence #2

Go back to the elevator and jump down - remember to hit the barrier using the Dash skill. Behind the green barrier, you will find the essence, thanks to which you will gain a lot of experience.

Databank #11 - Dead Jedi

Go through the obstruction and, bobbing off the wall in front, get to the top. There you will actually want to obtain another skill for BD-1. Then head to the furthest limit of the way and bounce down one level. When you step on the sheet metal floor, you will be dropped down.

Presently you'll have to locate a window with a green obstruction - overcome it.

You will wind up in a cavern with a bomb and a new databank section.

Treasure #7 - Datadisc

Nearby, by the skeleton, you will find another datadisc.

Databank #12 - A Fallen Knight

Grab the bomb nearby and destroy the barrier blocking the passage - behind it you will find an echo with another databank entry.

Databank #13 - Rayvis' Search

The following hindrance that you want to destroy is located a piece higher. Use a bomb and move up to the new passage.

There you will track down another bomb on the opposite wall. Destroy the following boundary. In the following room hack one of the doors. After a short walk, you will find another databank passage.

Databank #14 - Republic Control Room

Close to the previous collectible there is a wall, which you can move to get to a window with a green obstruction. You will find a PC that you can scan following helping through the hindrance.

Essence #3

In the wake of scanning the PC, hack the gadget in the room. You will get the It's a Snare prize and the locations of all chests will currently be put on the guide. From that point forward, leap to the edge above and use the entryway - behind it, to one side, you will find an essence that will increase the most extreme Power level.

Mountain Ascent

Mountain Ascent belongs to a bigger district, Prospector's Indiscretion, in the world Koboh. On this page of the manual for Star Wars: Jedi Survivor you will find descriptions of every one of the 18 secrets that can be gathered around there, including seed pods, treasures or databanks. You can get to Mountain Ascent by means of the Lower region Falls. While visiting for the second time, you can simply use fast travel.

List of secrets in Mountain Ascent

There are 18 collectiblesto find here:

- **Chests**: 6

- Databanks: 4
- Treasures: 4
- Seed Pods: 4

Databank #1 - Braving the Heights

Opposite the meditation point, you will find the first echo to listen to. This will, you will find a databank entry.

Treasure #1 - Priorite Shard

Go forward by jumping over the ledges under the waterfall, and you will reach the first treasure.

Seed Pod #1 - Koboh Spiker: Felucian Yellow

Nearby there's a small bush where you will get a seed pod.

Chest #1 - Bottoms: Bomber

Get back to the reflection point and afterward head to the green obstruction. Behind it, you will have the valuable chance to show BD-1 another skill. Head further, bounce down behind the second boundary and ultimately you will reach a chest with a cosmetic thing for Cal.

Seed Pod #2 - Koboh Spiker

To the right of the chest you will find a bush with another seed pod.

Chest #2 - Light Mustache and Patch

Return to the spot with the green barriers and afterward head to one side towards the gathering of enemies. You will end up by a small water reservoir (and a gadget to open a shortcut). At the lower part of the reservoir there's a chest with another sort of facial hair.

Databank #2 - Crashed Tie Fighter

Run up a nearby wall (which you can get to using a rope) and then walk ahead. You will reach a fighter wreck (down, next to the path), by which you'll get a databank entry.

Chest #3 - Jacket: Drifter

Near the wreckage there is a chest, which you have to lift and slam.

Databank #3 - Shiverpede Nest

Return up the slope to the way you took previously to arrive and watch out for a gathering of enemies. Prior to going higher, search for the entry to a small cavern. Inside it, there is an entryway which you must lift using your skill. You will get to a dull cavern with several enemies inside. Subsequent to battling them, you will track down a nest to scan.

Chest #4 - Mustache and Patch

Near the nest described above there is a chest containing a new beard for Cal.

Treasure #2 - Priorite Shard

Get back to the wall and run along it to jump onto the nearby ledge. You will make it easier for yourself by jumping off as late as possible, using double jump and the dash skill.

After that, you will get to a cave where you will find another Priorite Shard.

Databank #4 - Mountainside Hut

Get back to the edge from which you hopped into the previously mentioned cavern and go to a small structure. Close by there is a gadget which you can use to initiate a shortcut.

Seed Pod #3 - Koboh Spiker

To one side of the above-described cabin, you can leap to another edge. Up on the stone wall you will track down another plant with seeds - you will get to it by strolling along the green obstruction located behind a huge withered tree.

Chest #5 - Audio Sensors: Scrapyard

Continue to stroll towards the gathering of enemies on the other side. At the point when you manage them, divert toward the path from which you came. You will find walls that you can run along to get to the top.

At the top you will find a chest, the contents of which can be gotten by using the Lift and Slam skills.

Treasure #3 - Priorite Shard

Bounce down before the chest and stroll ahead. You will run over an entryway that you want to open with a wrench. Behind it, bounce down to a genuinely sizable square, where there is a major gathering of enemies (counting two bigger ones). After the battle, make a beeline for the wall, where you should get a cluster of stones to get the Priorite Shard out.

Seed Pod #4 - Koboh Spiker

The last portion of seeds in the area is relatively close, to the left side of the last collectible.

Treasure #4 - Priorite Shard

Going forward, you will see that you can get to a high ledge using a hook. There you will find another Priorite Shard.

Chamber of Detachment

How to reach the Chamber of Detachment?

You will help to the Chamber of Detachment through the Mountain Ascent. Starting from the reflection point around here, head towards the green barriers. Subsequent to overcoming the two of them, go directly ahead and afterward down. The entry to the chamber is taken cover behind a waterfall.

Some of the secrets must be accessed in the wake of finishing the last chapters of the game - the last skill required for them is opened in the course of the fifth part of the game.

List of secrets in the Chamber of Detachment

There are 6 collectiblesto find here:

- Chests: 1

- Essences: 1

Star Wars Jedi: Survivor: The Complete Official Guide & Walkthrough

- Databanks: 3
- Treasures: 1

Databank #1 - A Rare Find

After using the elevator, go straight ahead. There is an echo a little to the left, near the elevator.

Databank #2 - Missing in Action

After moving deeper in the chamber, head immediately to the right. You will find another echo.

Databank #3 - Worlds Away

This echo is in the opposite corner of the chamber, against the same wall.

Treasure #1 - Datadisc

To get the main treasure located here, you'll need to accomplish more work. Start by using the Power Pull several times on the huge block located close to the previous collectible. You will actually want to take the sphere concealed there.

Move it to the spot close to the second reverberation (Missing in real life). There you need to put it in a gadget that emits a laser bar.

Then you must use BD-1's skill and consume the dull development - like in the image above.

Chest #1 - Jedi Paint

You must use the previously mentioned block to consume the dim development, close to the entry to the chamber. Use BD-1 skill to cover the block in the substance so that it connects with the development. Then point it at the laser bar, so you can move it back and consume the development.

You will expose the second block, which should be pulled out. Behind it is a chest with a cosmetic component for BD-1.

Essence #1

To get to the essence, you need to put the two blocks generally in the center of the chamber - where there is a button in the floor.

This way you will actually want to move one of them to the lift located against the wall. At the point when you do this, eliminate the second block from the button and immediately hop on the one that is climbing. In this manner you will get higher.

The essence will give you another Advantage.

Fogged Expanse

List of secrets in the Fogged Expanse area

There are 24 secrets to be found:

- Chests: 3
- Essences: 2
- Databanks: 3
- Treasures: 7
- Seed Pods: 9

Treasure #1 - Priorite Shard

Starting from the contemplation point, head up the way toward the vines close to the edge. There, turn right and use the BD-1 skill on the fuse - this will bring the wall closer, and presently you can stumble into it.

Stroll ahead (in the interim overcoming a couple of enemies en route) until you reach a stone shelf, which you can reach with a rope with a snare. On it you will meet a small Droid snooping in the ground - be careful with a strong foe close by.

Databank #1 - Forging Forward Alone

Turn back and cross the metal bridge. You will find a wall to run through. After doing it, go straight and you will find the echo as well as the first entry in the database.

Essence #1

Get back to the metal structure and stand on a piece of the extension raised upwards - from that point you will actually want to see the essence on a slightly distant stage.

Before the entryway there is an essence that will give you a lot of involvement points.

Treasure #2 - Priorite Shard

Nearby, under a pile of stones, is another Priorite Shard. You have to use your lifting force to get him out.

Chest #1 - Material: Exile

To open the close by entryway and get to the chest, you'll have to use BD-1 on the fuse by the enormous fan close to the last secret you found.

Then head toward the reflection point by bouncing down to the edge beneath, yet instead of going to it, go to the back.

You will wind up in a small cavern, where's a chest in a lit region. On the manner in which you will meet a prospector.

Treasure #3 - Priorite Shard

Hold close to the edge head down the opposite path from the chest described previously. Then leap to a small shelf. Close to the skeleton is a Priorite Shard.

Treasure #4 - Priorite Shard

Head outside and head slightly off to one side and afterward stroll ahead into a more hazy region. Before you reach the destination showed on the guide above, you might experience a boss joined by Haxion's Brood Commando. You will track down a Priorite Shard under the stones.

Databank #2 - Monitoring Equipment

Head in the opposite direction to the last secret, and you will eventually reach a destroyed device that you can scan.

Chest #2 - Soul Patch

From the last passage in the database go down the front. You will find the walls, on which you can run further to the shelf with vines - you will get to the walls using a rope with a snare. In the wake of scaling, head directly down the way - toward the finish of the way you will track down a chest. Watch out for the part of mines that will show up.

Essence #2

From the one described above, hop down to the shelf beneath on the right. There, skip ahead, and you'll slide down a slippery street to an incredible rival, the Disgusting Bilemaw. Subsequent to battling it, you will actually want to use the essence, which will give you another Advantage.

Treasure #5 - Priorite Shard

There is a lift close by, which will permit you to get to the following secret and - open a shortcut. Subsequent to getting to the top, look towards the edge behind you - there is a small rock, close to which a Priorite Shard lies by the skeleton. There is an adversary close by.

Seed Pod #1 and #2 - Koboh Spiker: Alderaan Blue

Near the fragment described above are two bushes with seeds.

Seed Pod #3, #4 and #5 - Koboh Spiker

To the right of the previous bushes are three more.

Seed Pod #6 - Koboh Spiker

The seeds can be found on the path up in front of the elevator.

Databank #3 - A Deadly Encounter

Not a long way from the bush described above is an entryway, on which you must use the draw force. You will open the entry to the cavern, where you'll track down the last database passage nearby. Watch out for the adversary hiding inside.

Chest #3 - Pommel: Detachment

Go outside and use the vines at the top. After jumping off them, turn back. You'll see a chest which you must lift and smash.

Treasure #5 - Priorite Shard

Nearby you will find a wall that you can run on if you use the push power on it first. When jumping off it, be prepared to use a grappling hook. You will get to the platform where the balloon is located.

Use it to get to the top of the platform you were on a moment ago.

You will find a Priorite Shard on a boulder located in the bushes.

Treasure #7 - Priorite Shard

Use the balloon again and jump down to the platform on the left.

In the nest you will find Priorite Shard.

Seedbags #7, #8 and #9 - Koboh Spiker

Next to the previous secret are three bushes, from which you will get seeds.

Marl Cavern

How to get to the Marl Cavern

You can reach the Marl Cavern through the Fogged Expanse. Subsequent to reaching the reflection point in Fogged Expanse, stroll ahead and afterward use the moving wall, which can be enacted with a fuse by BD-1.

Then go straight until you reach the edge, which you can get to using a catching snare. Subsequent to getting on it, shift focus over to one side - there is another edge there that you can bounce on similarly.

Turn right at the first open door. You will go over an entryway, behind which there is a secret access to the cavern.

Some of the secrets must be accessed in the wake of finishing the last chapters of the game - the last skill required for them is opened during the fifth section of the game.

List of secrets in the Marl Cavern

There are **4 collectibles** to find here:

- Essences: 1
- Databanks: 1
- Force Tears: 1
- Treasures: 1

Databank #1 - Storage Tanks

You will find the first secret right at the entrance.

Treasure #1 - Priorite Shard

You will find the next secret after jumping down, right by the vines.

Force Tear #1 - Fractured Power

Use the vines to get back to the top. A little further you will find a fuse, which BD-1 should interface with. One of the walls will tumble down, permitting you to run further.

Toward the end, you should use a catching snare to safely land. You will also stumble upon an inflatable, with the use of which you will leap to the desired stage.

You will find a Power Tear called Cracked Power. The test consists in overcoming enemies.

Essence #1

Use the inflatable to get back to the top. Then run along the wall and when you're on the following stage, bounce onto the structure to one side of the fuse.

From that point, bounce onto the following walls and hurry to get to the high edge.

You will get to an essence, which will increase your HP level.

Imperial Post 8L-055

Star Wars Jedi: Survivor: The Complete Official Guide & Walkthrough

How to get to the Imperial Post 8L-055?

You will get to the Royal Post 8L-055 through Marl Cavern - you can figure out how to get to the cavern in the section committed to this area. When you're in the Marl Cavern, stroll ahead towards the walls and the fuse - using the BD-1 skill on the fuse will bring down the first wall, permitting you to get further through.

After a series of walls to run, you should use a rope with a snare to land. Subsequent to getting to the stage, turn around and you will see a wall that will get you to the following spot.

From that point, just go upstairs and afterward outside. This is where you'll experience a gathering of enemies and furthermore track down a rope to get into the desired area.

Some of the secrets must be accessed subsequent to finishing the last chapters of the game - the last skill required for them is opened during the fifth part of the game.

List of secrets in the Imperial Post 8L-055

There are 4 collectiblesto find here:

- Chests: 2

- Databanks: 2

Databank #1 - Abandoned Prospector Equipment

Subsequent to using the rope prompting the post and overcoming the soldiers, go for it. You will view the first items as scanned. Close by you'll track down a shortcut (a lift) to Fogged Expanse.

Chest #1 - Textured Rubber

Walk ahead using the grapple hook and vines until you reach the meditation point. From there, jump down onto a ledge a little lower and run ahead.

Get over the precipice and you will find a chest blocked by a fuse.

Databank #2 - Docking Clamp Overrides

Get back to the reflection point and go the other way. You will spot an old tree and a fuse behind it, on a structure, - shooting it will make the zipline emerge.

Subsequent to arriving on the mountain, go to the computers. You will get a databank passage.

Chest #2 - Barrel: RSKF-44

Go further by bouncing over the wall, then hop down to the extremely base using the platforms. There, use the lift.

Continuing on, you will ultimately run over the fuse located behind the fan. Subsequent to shooting at it, you will actually want to get further along the now accessible wall.

Continue to stroll ahead until you reach a vast room with a slope in the center. There, shift focus over to one side. You will see a chest in the close by room.

Summit Ridge

List of secrets in Summit Ridge

There are 8 collectibles to find here:

- Essences: 1

- Databanks: 2

- Treasures: 2

- Seed Pods: 3

Treasure #1 - Priorite Shard

Near the meditation point, by the elevator that opens the shortcut, you will find a Priorite Shard.

Databank #1 - Journey's End

To the right of the previous collectible, at the very edge, there is a databank entry.

Seed Pod #1 - Koboh Spiker

Go further using the balloon and go to the left on the next platform - you will find a seed bush there.

Essence #1

Go further by using the catching snare to get to the close by vines. Before you hop down in the following section, look slightly to one side, towards the inflatable dispensing gadget.

Snatch one and retreat by going for the gold the spot demonstrated in the picture above.

Subsequent to bouncing on the inflatable, promptly head to one side - you will see an entry to a cavern.

At the finish of the way you will track down the essence, from which you will get a lot of involvement.

Databank #2 - High-Altitude Research

Return and continue walking to the balloon device. You will be able to scan them, which will give you an entry in the databank.

Seed Pod #2 - Koboh Spiker

To the left of the previous collectible there is another seed pod.

Seed Pod #3 - Koboh Spiker

Then take the balloon and throw it towards the platforms shown in the screenshot above.

You will find another portion of seeds.

Treasure #2 - Datadisc

Stay on the same stage where you found the last seed case. Head forward and hop down to the inflatable gadget. Toss one towards a far off island, as seen in the screenshot above.

Subsequent to leaping off the inflatable, you will actually want to climb the vines to get to the top. There, under a heap of stones, you will find a datadisc.

Observatory Understructure

List of secrets in the Observatory Understructure

There are **8 collectibles** to find here:

- Chests: 2
- Databanks: 2
- Treasures: 2

Databank #1 - Erratic Dust

Starting from the meditation point, head downstairs and you will find an area to scan.

Treasure #1 - Datadisc

Return upstairs and go on from that point. As soon as you get out in the wake of climbing the edge, search briefly climbing surface on the right. Go to the furthest limit of the way and you will find a datadisc.

Treasure #2 - Datadisc

Then stroll ahead until you reach the primary, largest structure - the spot shown in the screenshot above. You can also perceive the perfect locations by the presence of shooting Droids in energy shields.

Once at the entry to the huge complex, shift focus over to one side. There is a chest from which you will actually want to bounce onto the roof of a close by building. There you will find a Droid, who has the datadisc that you really want to get.

Databank #2 - Forfeit Your Lives

Return and head the other way - there you should finish a series of challenges to get further.

The area of the databank passage in question is brimming with hostile Droids. You can track down a reverberation to listen to at one of the edges.

Chest #1 - Max Stims Increased

Starting where you tracked down the last collectible, head down the opposite path, towards the electric obstacle. When there, leap to the climbing wall using the launcher on an enormous turning structure.

Once at the top, go through the hole on the left. There, snatch an inflatable and toss it outside - in the wake of bouncing on it, promptly pivot to hop a level higher.

You will find a huge chest giving you an increase in the greatest furthest reaches of Stims.

Chest #2 - Grip: Showdown

Go to the room behind the chest and follow the way forward. You will go over a lift and an entryway on which you must use the Lift skill to go through them.

Then you should use the BD-1 skill on the fuse to open the entryway. Behind it, hop a little lower and look behind you, under the edge where you leaped off - you will actually want to see the stage, as shown in the screenshot above.

Subsequent to hopping down there, you will track down a chest.

Diagnostics Corridor

List of secrets in the Diagnostics Corridor

There are 5 collectibles to find here:

- Essences: 2

- Databanks: 2

- Treasures: 1

Databank #1 - Merciless Rampage

You will find the first databank passage at the absolute starting point of the area. At the point when you help to it through a small window (which you can open using the Lift skill), go promptly to one side - there is a reverberation you can listen to.

Databank #2 - Minor Oculus

Starting from the contemplation point, go to the round room where you can change the position of the open passage with a fuse. You will find a databank section in it.

Essence #1

In the room where you saw as the previous collectible, you must use the fuse until the opposite passage on the right side (looking from the reflection point) is open. Meanwhile, make a point to watch out for foe groups that might show up here.

Then go through the passage before you and bounce up - from that point, when you pivot, you will actually want to see the gadget distributing balloons.

Take one and toss it outside through a close by window. In the wake of hopping on it, make a beeline for the right, where you will view as another one.

Then head towards the window with the green obstruction. At the point when you traverse it, gaze upward - the essence you're searching for will be on a shelf. You can get to the top by hopping from the "windowsill" by the green obstruction.

In the wake of using the essence, you will increase as far as possible.

Treasure #1 - Datadisc

After collecting the essence, jump down. Directly below the previous collectible there is a datadisc lying on a couple of boxes.

Essence #2

To get to the second essence, you'll need to traverse the Observation Deck (or just use fast travel to the Fantastic Oculus). Subsequent to getting the previous collectible, you will actually want to open a shortcut prompting a gadget dispensing balloons - you were there prior.

Take one inflatable and toss it outside towards the metal mesh used for climbing. From it, leap to one side to exploit the shifting walls to run along them.

After you land safely, use the climbing matrix close to you. Once at the top, make a beeline for the right. You will experience a huge gathering of enemies.

In the wake of overcoming them, go to a high edge using a rope with a snare. You will end up in the Incomparable Oculus.

Feel free to use the lift in the center.

It will take you straightforwardly to the essence with another Advantage.

Observation Deck

List of secrets in the Observation Deck

There are 2 collectiblesto find here:

- Essences: 1
- Databanks: 1

Essence #1

Starting from the contemplation point in the Diagnostics Corridor, walk a piece ahead and you will see a round room with a fuse in the center and a portal at the top.

In the wake of using the trapdoor, you will wind up at the top, close to a wall canvassed in half with a climbing network.

In the wake of moving up, go to one side - you will actually want to see the essence, which will increase your HP.

Databank #1 - Grand Oculus

Subsequent to gathering the essence, return towards the seal and continue running, passing the energy-producing machine on the way.

Subsequent to climbing the network, rush to one side. An enormous gathering of opponents can be seen as here. Manage them and move toward the structure set apart in the screenshots above. You will get the just databank section accessible here. It is located extremely close to the Observation Deck's contemplation point, so you can get to it by starting there.

Rift Passage

How to get to the Rift Passage?

You can get to the Break Passage from the Observation Deck contemplation point. Starting on the Deck, go straight to the enormous lift. It will bring you down to the room with the essence.

Somewhat further on is another lift, which will bring you down to a corridor - go right to reach another lift, through which you will get to the Break Passage thus opening a shortcut.

Some of the secrets must be accessed in the wake of finishing the last chapters of the game - the last skill required for them is opened in the course of the fifth section of the game.

List of secrets in the Rift Passage

There are **2 collectibles** to find here:

- Chests: 1

- Treasures: 1

Treasure #1 - Datadisc

To reach the treasure, you must first leap to the high stage shown in the image above. You will do this by using a close by rope, and afterward doing a dash.

You'll track down a Datadisc on neighboring debris.

Chest #2 - Kashyyk Paints

Before you leap off the stage discussed above, take a gander at the chest beneath. Spot the fuse located between the rocks.

Use BD-1's skill, then rapidly leap to open the chest. You will get a cosmetic component for BD-1.

Viscid Bog

List of secrets in the area of the Viscid Bog

There are **13 collectibles** to find here:

- Chests: 3
- Essences: 1
- Databanks: 1
- Treasures: 1
- Seed Pods: 3

Databank #1 - Crashed Vulture Droid

Starting from the reflection site, check out peering down. You will actually want to spot an islet with a chest. Close to it is a disaster area to be scanned. This will acquire you the first section in the databank.

Chest #1 - Jacket: Drifter

As mentioned above, there is a chest next to the databank entry.

Databank #2 - Hastily abandoned site

Turn away from the above-described finds, and you will be able to see a tunnel in front of you.

Inside it, right at the entrance, is another databank entry.

Seedbag #1 - Crimson Jelly Spire: Alderaan Blue

Leave the passage and, being outside, use the catching snare to get to the top - over the last secret. From that point, make a beeline for the left and hop down. On the shore is a bush with seeds.

Seedbag #2 - Crimson Jelly Spire

For another batch of seeds, head to the right to climb higher up the wall there. The bush is located nearby.

Databank #3 - Risky business

Across from the bush is an echo with an entry in the databank.

Treasure #1 - Datadisc

In the area of the previous secret, you can locate a rock to climb higher. Then, following the only available path at the very top, you will reach a pile of stones, under which the databank is hidden.

Seedbag #3 - Crimson Jelly Spire

Get back to the reflection site - you will do this by raising the stage on the marsh and bouncing over it to the slope with the contemplation point.

On the same slope you will find a rope that will permit you to get to the following one mostly up (you must leap off at the right second). You'll need to land in the mud under a small cavern. From that point you will actually want to see the connection point for the catching snare.

While ashore, follow the main accessible way higher up to where the entry to one of the chambers is. Before it and by the steel bridge is the last part of seeds.

Databank #4 - Abominable Bogling

Return and skip to the previous one. Instead of getting back to the contemplation region, hop down into the swamp - you will soon see an anchor point for catching snare before you - and in the wake of leaping off the post, another one on the wall used for climbing.

When you're ashore, go to one side and you'll see a stage to raise in the swamp. Get and get around the following ones to get to the slope visible somewhere far off.

Star Wars Jedi: Survivor: The Complete Official Guide & Walkthrough

This will acquire you a passage in the databank.

Chest #2 - Stims amount increased

Proceed to the islet, where a huge rival is meandering near. A boss fight awaits you (an incredible rival named Mirre Fear). Subsequent to overcoming him, you will actually want to open a huge chest with Stim redesign.

Chest #3 - Activator: Persistence

Presently the main thing passed on to do is to return to where you tracked down the reverberation with the Detestable Swamp, and afterward to the slope from which you started leaping to the previously mentioned secret. There is a flying animal and a lift prompting the Dredger Gorge.

Exploit the lift and sooner or later leap out of it through an opening in the wall - pay special attention to the second when it brightens up a piece from the sunlight. Subsequent to getting ashore, head down and back and you will track down a chest.

Databank #5 - Sights Set

Take advantage of the three balloons in the area and you will get to the last databank entry in the area.

Essence #1

Take hold of the flying animal and fly ahead until you reach the balloons, yet keep to the left (the ones on the right are excessively high for the time being).

Get around additional balloons until you are at last compelled to get around a rope - and from it almost quickly to a close by expand. Soon you will have the chance to contact the ground.

You will find an essence that will increase the greatest HP level.

Chamber of Connection

List of secrets in the Chamber of Connection

There are **7 collectibles** to be found:

- Chests: 1
- Essences: 1
- Databanks: 4
- Treasures: 1

Databank #1 - Homesick

After descending into the chamber, head immediately to the left towards the wall - there you will find an echo with a databank entry.

Chest #1 - Emitter: Persistence

To get to the main chest accessible in this area, you must proceed and stand on the button - this will make the way for a storage room with a circle.

Snatch the circle and use it on the laser shaft gadget located close to the lift you showed up in at the chamber. From that point forward, you should simply use the BD-1 processor, guiding it to the vines to your left side (the more distant one; let the heading of the laser bar assist you with this). En route, stay away from the water - further on, you should direct the processor as close to the wall as possible.

You will discover a chest taken cover behind the vines. There is a cosmetic thing for the lightsaber.

Treasure #1 - Datadisc

While getting to the chest described above, you needed to destroy the vines - behind them there is another passage. Exploit it and promptly go to the wall on the right. In the wake of hopping up thanks to it, you will go over a datadisc.

Databank #2 - Insolence, or Bravery

After heading to the right of the last collectible, you will be able to notice arather tall structure on the opposite side of the chamber. Hop on it, then stand on the button.

Note that there is another button at the flip side of the structure - both will be useful in a second.

Presently you want to use the BD-1 processor and guide the stream to one side, while standing on the previously mentioned buttons when it's required (this way you will bypass the waterfall that prevents you from using the processor).

This will open another passage.

Behind the new passage, there's the main passage that will take you to the following databank section.

Databank #3 - Mind Challenge

After collecting the above entry, jump down to the platform below on the right. Walk forward a bit further and you will come across another echo.

Essence #1

In the wake of gathering the collectible described above, open the close by entryway. Then bounce down and start driving the BD-1 processor through the previously opened passage and upstairs - just as we described toward the finish of the Chamber of Connection page. At last you will find a room with an essence that will give you another advantage.

Databank #4 - Private Doubts

In the same room, in the corner on the left looking from the previous collectible, there is a databank entry.

Loading Gantry

List of secrets in the Chamber of Connection

There are **12 collectibles** to find here:

- Chests: 5
- Databanks: 3
- Treasures: 4

Databank #1 - Sunken AAT

Starting from the contemplation point, go to squeeze through the hole in the opposite entryway. On the other side, you will be gone after by a rather huge gathering of enemies. The databank section is located not a long way from the passage, precisely before it.

Chest #1 - Short Goatee

In the wake of gathering the section described above, go to one side and leap to the other side. There, go to the furthest limit of the huge stage. Once more, you should overcome several enemies. In the chest you will track down another facial hair for Cal.

Treasure #1 - Priorite Shard

There are enormous containers and devices nearby - Priorite Shard will lie on one of them. Circumventing the containers, you will find a chest that will permit you to get higher. At the point when you're going to bounce on the last one, don't attempt to do it by standing as close to it as possible - step away a little.

Databank #2 - Brave New World

Go to the opposite end of the platform you are standing on and use a grappling hook to get to the wall. Climb to the top and from there, jump to the structure on the left. There is a databank entry.

Databank #3 - Storage Tanks

Afterwards, you really want to go to the start of the area and head towards the lift (it's smart to open it for the future collectible searches - you can do it in Storage Rafters, the following area). Close to the lift you'll find a databank passage.

Treasure #2 - Priorite Shard

Behind the previously scanned tanks you will find a Priorite Shard.

Chest #2 - Material: Commander

Then use the enormous lift. When you are at the top, shift focus over to one side, where you will actually want to see a fuse - use the BD-1 Electro Dart on it. Close to the fuse there is an edge, which you can access using a catching snare You will track down a chest there.

Treasure #3 - Priorite Shard

Head towards the meditation point and jump down - under the sloping passage to the top you will find a Priorite shard.

Chest #3 - Barrel: Enforcer

While on the same level, close to the reverberation (not included as a collectible in this area), you will track down a trapdoor at the top. Run sideways on the walls and overcome the green obstruction.

There are several enemies on the other side. In the wake of overcoming them, run on the walls to one side - watch out for the current, which will lose you assuming that you contact it.

Subsequent to landing, hop down to the stage showed previously.

You will find a chest there.

Treasure #4 - Priorite Shard

Get some distance from the previously opened chest and make a beeline for the right - you will track down a wall to move close to the green obstruction.

In the wake of traversing it, rout the enemies and turn left before the entryway. A piece further on you will run over another shard.

Chest #4 - Grip: Persistence

Pivot and gaze directly ahead. There is a wall which you can use to hop higher. On the right, notwithstanding, there are green barriers and walls to run on.

You will find more walls, which will get you higher. At the top, you will track down a chest.

Chest #5 - Jacket: Commander

A bit further on you will see walls to run on. Run ahead using them.

After overcoming a series of challenges, you will end up on land near a chest.

Star Wars Jedi: Survivor: The Complete Official Guide & Walkthrough

Lucrehulk Core

List of secrets in the Lucrehulk Core

There are 9 collectibles to find here:

- Chests: 2

- Essences: 2

- Databanks: 3

- Treasures: 2

Databank #1 - The Origins of Purpose

Starting from the reflection point called Shed Rafters, head through the opposite entryway. Then follow the long corridor - there are no expanding paths or rooms while heading to your destination. In any case, you will experience opponents en route. In the long run, you will reach a collapse that you can squeeze through.

Then head to one side, where you will track down a reverberation with a databank passage.

Databank #2 - A New Master

Return a piece to the breach in the wall - you will see green barriers.

Go through them and you will reach a spot with moving containers. Take hold of one of them and hold on until you are dropped - then rapidly get to the ground.

Being at the base, you will be gone after by a gathering of opponents. After the battle, head up the close by stairs and afterward use the lift in the following room. You will go even lower.

Use the contemplation point called the Lucrehulk Core.

Go left of the contemplation point - toward the stopping point you will see a reverberation with a databank section.

Chest #1 - Photoreceptors: Geonosian

Get back to the contemplation point. Standing close to it, focus on the left - there are two platforms on the wall that you can go all over. Raise the one on the right higher, and the one on the left should be moved lower. Then hop on the right one and immediately get to the left stage - it is going up, so you have restricted time.

At the top you will track down the chest.

Essence #1

Subsequent to opening the chest, bounce down to the platforms you associated with before and go to one side to hop down. Then go straight for some time and go right at the first turn - watch out for the turret on the roof.

Then stroll towards the way behind the turret and hop down to the shelf underneath shown in the above screenshot.

You will go over additional turrets - there is an entryway you can raise close to one of them.

Behind the entryway you will find an essence that will provide you with a great deal of involvement.

Treasure #1 - Priorite Shard

Return to the green boundary you as of late passed. Get past it and afterward cross the space to the bridge. There is a messed up railing in the bridge - bounce towards the stage visible from that spot.

You will track down a Priorite Shard.

Treasure #2 - Priorite Shard

Return to the bridge and run to its end. After crossing it, you will encounter a small Droidholding a Priorite Shard. Catch him before he escapes and watch out for ceiling turrets.

Chest #2 - Pommel: Persistence

After collecting the Priorite Shard from the fleeing Droid, jump over the precipice toward the place from where the turrets fired. There's a chest there, which you'll open using Force Lift and Slam skills.

Databank #3 - Look On My Works

Return to the main road and continue walking. After a while, you will come across an echo with a databank entry.

Essence #2

Move higher to one side of the last collectible - this way you will actually want to open a shortcut. Then return to the reflection point. Opposite it is a lift, which you must draw down using the fitting skill.

In the wake of using it, quickly go to one side and go the whole way to the end. You will find an essence that will increase your HP level.

Forward Control Tower

List of secrets in Forward Control Tower

There are **5 collectibles** to find here:

- Chests: 1
- Essences: 1
- Databanks: 2
- Treasures: 1

Chest #1 - Center Part

Regardless of whether you got to the area by fast travel or through an enormous lift (located in the Lucrehulk Core), you need to go to one side - be mindful so as not to start the lift by standing in the center, because then you should ride as far as possible. In the space to one side of the lift you will find a chest, which you will open using the lift and Power Slam skill.

Essence #1

Starting from the reflection point, go to the corridor visible on the left and in the following room, go through the separated window to leap to the huge round stage. There you will find the essence that will give you another Advantage.

Databank #1 - Escape Pod

After collecting the essence, use the hook line to get to the broken passage opposite. Being at the top, head to the right and go all the way to the door - at the end of the room you will find a databank entry.

Databank #2 - Emergency Landing

Return to the meditation point and head down the corridor beyond. There is an echo with a databank entry.

Treasure #1 - Priorite Shard

There is a seal on the roof close to the reflection point. Use it and walk straight, and inevitably you will reach a hole through which you can squeeze.

You will stand over the incline, where you can see the wall to be moved higher - set it at the right level and afterward stumble into it.

Then, you should adjust the plates likewise. Bob off them to get to the high shelf on the right.

At the point when you get higher, move the plates to make them significantly higher. From them you will get to the wall above - set apart in the above screenshot.

Hop from the first wall to the second - the Need Shard is located in it. Luckily, everything you need to do is raced to it - you don't need to push anything.

Yurt Barracks

List of secrets in the Yurt Barracks

There are 12 collectibles to find here:

- Chests: 3

- Essences: 3

- Databanks: 3

- Treasures: 3

Essence #1

Starting from the Lucrehulk Core contemplation point, go down the way to one side and use the entryway in the following corridor - you'll reach the Yurt Barracks. In the wake of passing through the entryway head right, then turn left toward the finish of the corridor to move higher.

When you get a piece higher, pivot - you'll see your level headed behind the messy windows.

Watch out for the unbelievable rival you'll look here - The Massiff. After the fight, use the essence to obtain lots of involvement.

Databank #1 - Bedlam Raider Yurt

In the wake of gathering the essence, hop down to where you've moved up from. Cross the passageway and continue onward on ahead, turning right two times. You'll reach an enormous square with a tent - the databank section is inside it.

Databank #2 - Location is Everything

Not far from the tent described above you'll find another databank echo.

Databank #3 - One's Man Junk

In the same square there's a wrecked entryway you can squeeze through. Behind it there's a wall thanks to which you can move higher up - at the exceptionally top leap off to one side to safely land.

At a more elevated level you'll track down the last database passage here. Watch out for the foe who'll go after as you pass the previously mentioned entryway.

Treasure #1 - Priorite Shard

Turn toward the wall you've been climbing and you'll spot a platform opposite to it. Jump on it to grab the Priorite Shard.

Chest #1 - Grip: Enforcer

After collecting the Priorite, look right - there's another platform you can jump on. You'll find a chest there.

Treasure #2 - Priorite Shard

Jump down to the roof of a nearby tent, then make your way to the next tent and climb higher.

There's a yet another tent at the top. Inside are two enemies and a Priorite Shard.

Chest #2 - Body: Geonosian

Leave the tent and bounce down a level beneath. Head further down a tight passage until you reach a pit.

From here leap to one side, to the room with a chest. Inside is a cosmetic component for BD-1.

Treasure #3 - Priorite Shard

In the wake of opening the previously mentioned chest, hop down to the square underneath - there should be numerous Pandemonium Raiders and some tents here.

Whenever you've managed them, return to the starting mark of the square and look right (from the side from which you came). You should spot an intensely lit way. From that point you can hop down to the shelf underneath.

Presently leap to the opposite shelf to track down the last Priorite Shard nearby.

Essence #2

Return to the camp and tent square and head left to the door you'll need to lift open. Behind it there's some essence which will give you lots of experience.

Essence #3

Get back to the square and proceed as soon as you arrive - there's a zipline there, from a previously activates shortcut. At the point when you're at the top, glance the way where you came from - you should see a high up shelf.

When you get on it, look left and you'll spot another one. There's an essence there, which will increase your greatest HP.

Chest #3 - Body: Enforcer

Get back to the previously mentioned shortcut and this time return, circumventing one of the transporters from the left and following the way prompting the top. You'll find a chest that must be opened with a fuse - the fuse is opposite the chest, high up on the wall.

Generator Underbelly

How to reach the Generator Underbelly?

You can reach this spot from the Yurt Barracks. Make a beeline for the put shown on the guide and bounce towards the mass of the shaft at the base. Cal will slide down on his sword. You can also use fast travel. Our aide explains where to find the seven secrets concealed here - the chest, the treasures and the essence.

Some of the secrets must be accessed subsequent to finishing the last chapters of the game - the last skill required for them is opened during the fifth part of the game.

List of secrets in the Generator Underbelly

There are **7 collectibles** to find here:

- Chests: 1

- Essences: 1

- Databanks: 3

- Treasures: 2

Databank #1 - Landing Hydraulics

Starting from the area's meditation point, look for a rope over a pit. Use it and after a while jump down to the platform. You'll find the databank entry there.

Essence #1

Using the stage where you've gotten the databank section, go as far as possible on the opposite side. You'll find a liftable block that will allow you to get higher.

Afterwards, pivot and you'll spot a wall thanks to which you can climb considerably higher.

A piece farther away is a stage you can lower and hop on - you should spot the essence somewhere far off.

From the brought down stage you can now get on the walls and reach the essence to increase your Power level.

Treasure #1 - Priorite Shard

Get back to where you've spotted the wall you've bounced on. Instead of climbing it once more, use the climbing framework on the other side - there's an Uproar Plunderer a piece further away.

However a piece further there's a mesh you must lower and climb. There's a single enemy here. However, not far away is another mesh you must raise and climb - it falls down after a brief while.

In the wake of using the mesh to go right, you'll spot another one you really want to leap to - there's another Madhouse Thief at the base. Close by is another mesh for you to lift. Behind it is the way forward.

When you reach the shelf, you can get the Priorite Shard.

Databank #2 - A Droid Reborn

Get back to the square where you battled the Pandemonium Looter and go to the edge - you'll see a stage underneath.

You'll have to set the close by grates at a right level to reach the edge presented previously.

Then head left, to a small room. The databank section is in a difficult spot. There are a couple of enemies close by.

Chest #1 - Slice: BX Droids

Close by is a fuse, which you will use to open the entryway under.

A piece further are three huge slabs you can use to rush to the other side - watch out for the Droid there. When you're on the other side, run along the same walls yet in the opposite bearing - your destination is the higher shelf.

You will find a gadget BD-1 can hack. This will show it another skill.

Treasure #2 - Priorite Shard

Run on the slabs again and head left once you're done. After jumping to the next platform you'll find a Priorite Shard.

Databank #3 - Power Generator

Get once again to the spot from where you can leap to the walls. There's a lift close by you must lower using Slam.

At the top you'll experience a boss (Hytho Pixx). Subsequent to overcoming the boss, go to the close by generator.

Boiling Bluff

List of secrets in the Boiling Bluff

There are 6 collectibles to find here:

- Databanks: 2

- Treasures: 2

- Seed Pods: 2

Databank #1 - The Wheel Turns

Starting from the contemplation point, locate any mount. While on its back, bounce onto a stone shelf close to the contemplation point. At the top you will track down the reverberation.

Treasure #1 - Priorite Shard

Get back on your mount and head into the nearby cave. Slightly to the right of the entrance is a wall - you'll get up it by jumping off the creature's back.

Databank #2 - Turgle, saved

Turn around - even before you jump down you should spot an echo holding a database entry.

Seed Pod #1 and #2 - Crimson Jelly Spire: Dathomirian Red

There are two plants nearby, from which you can get the seeds.

Treasure #2 - Priorite Shard

Get back to the cavern entrance close to the reflection point, yet don't as yet leave. Turn upward instead, you should spot some distinctive walls. One of them (the one to one side) holds a Priorite Shard.

Reaching them starting from the earliest stage is troublesome, or even impossible. You can use a small point of support close by - bounce on it with your mount, leap off the mount and dash in mid-air. Then skip off the first wall and get the shard as you're sliding during the time one.

Swindler's Wash

Swindler's Wash - list of secrets

There are **18 collectibles** to find here:

- Chests: 2

- Essences: 1

- Force Tears: 1

- Treasures: 3

- Seed Pods: 11

Seedpod #1 - Goldenlight Moss: Nabooan Green

There are a few interactable plants near the meditation point. The first one is at the wall.

Seedpod #2 - Goldenlight Moss

Found near the meditation point.

Seedpod #3 - Goldenlight Moss

For Seedbag #3, you'll need to go a little further and jump to a shelf on the other side of the chasm. The plant is at the edgeof the shelf.

Chest #1 - Tactical Pants

Get back to the contemplation point and continue straight forward to reach a cavern somewhat further ahead.

When there, go on until you reach a limited opening driving outside. There are some enemies to overcome here. The chest is on the water.

Treasure #1 - Priorite Shard

In the wake of purging the previous chest, hop down and continue toward the waterfall seen somewhere far off. Enormous adversary will intrude on your walk forward.

When you rout him, run up the wall to get upstairs. Presently pivot and run up another wall considerably higher.

The Priorite Shard is in the cavern.

Essence #1

After collecting the Shard, go back outside and once again run up the wall to get higher. You should see the Essence in the distance.

Collecting the essence is rewarded with a large XP boost.

Treasure #2 - Priorite Shard

From the area where you've found the Essence, you can see another "post" in front of you. Jump on it, and you'll find Priorite Shard #2.

Seedpod #4 - Goldenlight Moss

Subsequent to gathering Priorite Shard #2, leap to the close by shelf tracked down slightly off to one side. After a little walk, you should see the plant. It is viewed as not a long way from a metal bridge which would lead (on the off chance that it wasn't destroyed) to a reflection point.

Treasure #3 - Priorite Shard

Proceed with the way that drove you to the plant, however this time turn left and leap to a higher shelf - you should reach a small cavern covered with hanging plants. Inside there is a Priorite Shard, the last one from this district. There will be 2 enemies to overcome en route.

Chest #2 - Tactical Shirt

In the neighborhood, at the edge, there is a chest - also the final one from this region.

Seedbags #5-8 - Pine Fern

There are 4 plants of the sought type on the left from the chest.

Seed Pod #9 - Spine Fluff

For this plant, you really want to descend to the extremely base, until you get yourself almost straightforwardly underneath the opened chest (Chest #2). The plant is by the stream.

Seed Pod #10 - Spine Fluff

From the previous Spine Fluff location, go left to find another seedpod.

Seed Pod #11 - Spine Fluff

Go further left, and climb a shelf, from which you really want to leap to the opposite shelf that is significantly higher. The last bunch of seeds is there.

Search for a waterfall. Behind it there is a small cavern with the Power Tear. The associated challenge involves some troublesome platforming. More data on Tears and associated challenges can be found in All Power Tears section of the aide, while this instance is definite in Cracked Resolve #1 page of the aide.

Basalt Rift

Basalt Rift - list of secrets

There are **23 collectibles** to find here:

- Chests: 5
- Databanks: 8
- Treasures: 5
- Seed Pods: 5

Seed Pod #1 - Goldenlight Moss

Once you enter Basalt Rift and proceed forward a little, you'll come across a zipline stretched over a chasm. Don't use it, but instead reach the platform on the left. The seeds are at its edge.

Treasure #1 - Priorite Shard

After collecting Seedpod #1, destroy the nearby column to discover a Priorite Shard.

Databank #1 - Basalt Pillars

In the wake of gathering Treasure #1 return to the zipline you've experienced and ride it. There is a scannable segment not a long way from where you've handled that adds another database section.

Seed Pod #2 - Goldenlight Moss

Not far from Databank #1, there is a plant.

Treasure #2 - Priorite Shard

Track down a small river and go upriver by running on walls above it - sadly, endeavoring to go upstream at the ground level doesn't work, as Cal slips with each endeavor.

At the point when you reach your destination, pivot and stumble into another wall, taking you significantly higher.

The Priorite Shard is in the upper region.

Databank #2 - Turf Wars

Subsequent to gathering Shard #2, leap to the lower edge and go through an opening.

Back outside, follow the way to one side and descend significantly further. At the edge before a chasm, you can see some vines somewhere out there, which can be reached by using the Ascension Link.

When on the other side, go right - you'll be a witness to a battle between two enemies. Stand by or step directly into the fight, then scan the close by structure. You will get a databank passage.

Databank #3 - Same Story, Different Planet

From Databank #2 area, continue left toward the cavern and a wall covered with vines - you can reach it by using the Ascension Link.

You'll reach an enormous region with a gathering of enemies. Rout them and you'll have the option to scan a reverberation that adds another database passage.

Chest #1 - Hunter Shirt

From Databank #3 area, pivot - you'll be before a chasm. There, you can see a dull cavern underneath. You can access it by using the Ascension Link.

The chest with an appearance thing is inside.

Databank #4 - Bilemaw's Revenge

Get back to Databank #3 area and this time head forward. Soon, you'll need to ride a steep slope and hop over a chasm.

When on the other side, you'll have to overcome one enormous rival and a gathering of lesser ones. In the wake of overcoming the opponents, you can scan the region from where the bigger adversary arose.

Chest #2 - Hunter Pants

Chest #2 is in the cave which entrance you've scanned moments ago.

Databank #5 - Risk and Research

Left from the cavern exit is a stage - from it, you can slide the first stone block out of the wall. Hop on the first block and slide out another one until a runnable wall is made - run the total wall and climb the vines to reach the upper region.

There is a camp here, and the databank is close by.

Seed Pod #3 - Goldenlight Moss

A plant is also in this area.

Treasure #3 - Datadisc

Leave the place to stay, and destroy the close by segment, which will make a shortcut back to the contemplation point. From the section, go left and proceed for some time until you reach an intersection. Follow the left corridor.

You'll experience a huge foe that you really want to overcome. In the wake of overcoming him, start climbing close by walls until you reach some vines.

The datadisc is on the upper level.

Chest #3 - Max Stims Increased

From the datadisc location, start going forward and turn right at the junction. After a short walk, you will come across a large chest containing the stim upgrade.

Chest #4 - Crew Cut

From Chest #3 area, hop down and follow the descending way - you'll pass some disintegrated columns, however proceed with the way and leap to the following edge beneath. You should experience a gathering of opponents - this is your destination.

When the region is clear, you can send BD-1 to open the chest. Inside there is another appearance thing - hairstyle.

Databank #6 - The Short Straw

Star Wars Jedi: Survivor: The Complete Official Guide & Walkthrough

The database entry is in the same area.

Treasure #4 - Priorite Shard

From Chest #4 and Databank #6 locations, descend even more. If while standing at the edge you'll look down, you should see a small droid holding the treasure. Eliminate him as fast as you can, preferably by surprise.

Chest #5 - Dilligence Pommel

Not a long way from the droid region, there is a cavern entrance. Chest #5 is inside. All you need to do in the wake of entering the cavern is turn left before the other side entry.

Databank #7 - Bilemaw Pools

Exit the cave and walk a little forward. The databank is next to the streams.

Seed Pod #4 - Goldenlight Moss

From Databank #7 location, look for a sleeping Bilemaw. The plant you're looking for is right next to him.

Seed Pod #5 - Goldenlight Moss

Another, final seedpod is in the same area.

Treasure #5 - Datadisc

To reach the last Treasure, you'll have to do some climbing. The ledges for the ascension are made through blocks in the wall that can be slid out by using Power Pull.

When you are at the top, use the way driving down, however watch out for dangerous matter at the bodies. Keep proceeding until you reach hanging vines (we show the spot in the screenshot above).

Use the vines to move beneath the roof and reach the finish of this way. The treasure (datadisc) you're searching for is in the cavern.

Databank #8 - Koboh Dust

Star Wars Jedi: Survivor: The Complete Official Guide & Walkthrough

From Treasure #5 location, return to the ceiling vines and go the opposite way. The vines will lead you to a metal structure from which you can jump down to a ledge. Once on the ledge, scan away.

Chamber of Reason

Chamber of Reason - list of secrets

There are **8 collectibles** to find here:

- Chests: 1

- Essences: 1

- Databanks: 5

- Treasures: 1

Databank #1 - The Goals of Khri

Subsequent to riding the lift and ending up in the chamber, use the zipline. Instead of riding it right down, search for a stage and leap to it, and from that point squeeze through an opening. In the wake of arising on the other side, turn left right away - the reverberation and database passage is there.

Databank #2 - Talk of the Future

Turn right and head all the way to the end and jump to the platform below. Another echo is here.

Databank #3 - Dead End

Getting to the Databank #3 area will see you solve some puzzles. They include moving spheres to speaker devices and making bridges - more on the riddle can be found on Chamber of Reason page of our aide. When you're at the top and approach the second sphere, open up a way to the reverberation seen somewhere far off.

Databank #4 - In Good Time

Star Wars Jedi: Survivor: The Complete Official Guide & Walkthrough

From Databank #3 location, look to your right for a platform. There is a runnable wall before it - use it to reach the upper level. After getting upstairs, look to the right corner and you'll find the echo.

Databank #5 - A Secret Meeting

From Databank #4 location, stay close to the wall and proceed in the opposite direction. You'll quickly reach another echo.

Treasure - Datadisc

Stay at the upper level and go straight ahead - at the very edge, there will be a treasure.

Chest: Lightsaber Emitter - Diligence

Return to the last sphere intensifier and move the switch close by. This will start a lift.

Take the sphere from the enhancer and toss it toward the path seen in the above screenshot. Be that as it may, you want to do it in such a manner so the sphere falls to the base. You'll figure out that you've made the right toss when a mesh seen beneath the round window will open.

Use the close by pathway and travel through the corridor to track down the chest.

Essence - Dexterity

The last secret is found by tossing the sphere somewhat further forward, to the intensifier. This and remaining puzzles in the zone are described in more detail on the previously mentioned Chamber of Reason page. At the point when gathered, the Essence unlocks Ability perk.

Forest Array

List of secrets in the Forest Array

There are **25 collectibles** to find here:

- Chests: 6

- Essences: 2

Star Wars Jedi: Survivor: The Complete Official Guide & Walkthrough

- Databanks: 6
- Treasures: 10
- Seed Pods: 1

Databank #2 - Orb Amplifier

The first databank is acquired during the main storyline. The second is in the same place, straight from the meditation point. Scan the Orb Amplifier to get it.

Chest #1 - Material: Hunter

Get back to the reflection point and head right, to the projecting piece of construction. From that point you can spot a hook point on the climbable mesh.

Climb it and go to track down the chest.

Treasure #1 - Datadisc

Return to the meditation point and head towards the protruding element on the other side - the treasure's at the bottom. Jump down, pick it up ASAP and go back up to score the Datadisc.

Databank #3 - Epic Moltings

In the wake of getting back to the top, go on, getting around platforms and reaching a mesh you can climb. You can open a shortcut there.

Continue to feel free to once you're past the locked entryway bounce onto the mesh.

While strolling along the mesh high up, bounce down at the first open door. A piece further ahead is a scannable region.

Chest #2 - Light Mustache

Go on ahead, running along the wall to reach the aforementioned locked door - you can now open it from the other side. The chest is on a high shelf in a round room nearby. Reach it by jumping off the wall and using the bar.

Databank #4 - Auxiliary Array Telescope

Keep going until you reach a small scannable building.

Chest #3 - Switch: Diligence

Next to the previous collectible is a climbable grate. At the top is yet another chest.

Essence #1

Return towards the network you've just leaped off. From that point you can spot a protrusion over the pit. Stand on it.

You'll spot an edge you can hook towards. The Essence should be visible somewhere off somewhere far off.

Reach it through another mesh. You'll be compensated with a lot of involvement.

Chest #4 - Material: Hunter

Not a long way from the previously mentioned Essence is a passage prompting previously visited areas. Subsequent to opening another shortcut, go right. Then head back to where you found the Databank #3. You should spot a chest nearby. Get around the dust pit to reach it.

Treasure #2 - Datadisc

Go ahead and fly forward with the help of a flying creature. Then run back. You'll find the Datadisc at the edge.

Treasure #3 - Datadisc

You'll require a sphere to get this treasure. Get one - ideally the one close to the furthest limit of the locations prompting the Recovery Wing. The Datadisc is close to a sleeping Bilemaw. You can reach it by holding a sphere shielding you from the dangerous dust.

Treasure #4 - Datadisc

Take the orb to the dust square on the opposite side. There's a withered tree nearby, with another Datadisc next to it. Approach it while holding the orb.

Databank #5 - Central Rotational Apparatus

Once again, take the orb and use the device in the large square next to the meditation point. Scan the mechanism for another databank entry.

Chest #5 - Grip: Diligence

Rotate the mechanism until the laser reveals the way to the chest.

Treasure #5 - Datadisc

Take out the orb and head into the dust. Another Datadisc lies on the plank.

Treasure #6 - Datadisc

Place the orb in the mechanism and rotate it towards the meditation point. You'll find the treasure at the square exit. Watch out for enemies nearby.

Treasure #7 - Datadisc

Since the laser beam is now hitting the stairs, you can use BD-1's Koboh Grinder to acquire the next nearby Datadisc. It is in a nearby growth.

Treasure #8 - Datadisc

Another Datadisc is on the edge of the platform near the customization workbench.

Treasure #9 - Datadisc

Another Datadisc is in a similar place to the previous one, but on the opposite side.

Treasure #10 - Datadisc

You must reach the top of a round room near the workbench. The treasure is on one of the platforms.

Chest #6 - Head: Swooper

Subsequent to gathering the Datadisc, bounce down towards the shortcut-opening gadget, then even lower onto the way. After a short walk you'll track down a dim fissure. Squeeze through it and Power Push an item to open the way onto a close by structure.

After jumping on it, go right to reach the chest.

Essence #2

Stay on the structure and go the other way until you reach the end. You'll see a couple of bars you can use to bounce further. Subsequent to using the second bar, get the rope to reach solid ground. After a short walk you'll reach the Essence and gain another advantage.

Seedpod - Goldenlight Moss

After collecting the essence, jump down to the front and head right. There's an enemy and a plant holding seeds. You'll find it to the left of the wooden platform.

Databank #6 - Indomitable

Travel toward the path opposite to where you've tracked down the last collectible and follow the left way (the better-lit one). Continue to feel free to get around the dust towards the structure close to the street on the right. Watch out for a gathering of enemies close by.

When on the structure, head left into the round room. There are more enemies here, as well as a scannable region to one side.

Rehabilitation Wing

Rehabilitation Wing - list of secrets

There are **2 collectibles** to find here:

- Essences: 1

- Databanks: 1

Essence

Starting from the meditation point, head forward to the main room. The Essence is at the edge - collecting it gives Cal a large XP boost. In the room, you may also encounter an optional boss called Yupah.

Databank - Beyond the Abyss

From Essence area, head outside and turn left toward the rail. Stroll across it and you'll reach a zipline gadget - enacting it unlocks a shortcut. The reverberation you're searching for is correct close by. This is one of the bigger echoes, resulting in a ton of XP acquired.

Bilemaw Den

Bilemaw Den - list of secrets

There are **3 collectibles** to find here:

- Chests: 1
- Essences: 1
- Seed Pods: 1

Essence - Confusion: Major Fauna

The Essence is in a dark cave found nearby the meditation point. Collecting it unlocks a new ability that allows confusing large animals.

Chest - Jacket: Tactical

Take the street that leads up and follow it until you reach a settlement. The chest is behind one of the small tents (close by a couple of balloons looming over a chasm). En route, you'll experience a huge foe bunch, joined by a Bilemaw.

Seedpod - Goldenlight Moss

Follow the only possible way and you should soon reach a waterfall. The plant you're looking for is right nearby.

Nekko Pools

List of secrets in Nekko Pools

There are 6 collectibles to find here:

- Chests: 1
- Databanks: 1
- Treasures: 2
- Seed Pods: 2

Treasure #1 - Priorite Shard

Go to a small cave located a little bit further from the meditation point, exactly opposite from it. There you will find a Priorite Shard.

Treasure #2 - Priorite Shard

Get on the mount and head to the passage next to the one from the previously described collectible. Keep going straight, and eventually you will reach the second and last Priorite Shard here.

Seed Pod #1 - Bluebell Squish

After leaving the cave with the shard, head left to a slightly larger square. There you will find a plant with seeds.

Databank - Nekko Scratches

Databank entry is to the left of the plant described above.

Seed Pod #2 - Bluebell Squish

In the same square there is a second portion of seeds, also against a wall.

Chest - Body: Swooper

Make a beeline for the reflection point and mount a Nekko on the way. At the point when you're there, head up the steep way close by.

After a short trip and a couple of jumps you will actually want to spot the entry to the cavern. Use Nekko to arrive (it's all in all too high for Cal himself).

Reach the finish of the way - there is a carton with a cosmetic thing for BD-1 close to the edge.

Bygone Settlement

List of secrets in the Bygone Settlement area

There are **15 collectibles** to find here:

- Chests: 4
- Essences: 1
- Databanks: 2
- Treasures: 5
- Seed Pods: 3

Database #1 - Ancient Architecture

Starting from the contemplation chamber, instead of hopping down, make a beeline for the right. You will actually want to spot a grinding you can climb.

At the point when you reach the roof, take hold of it and push ahead as far as possible. Toward the end, hop down to the footbridge close to the structure.

Walk straight until you reach the end. You will find the databank section.

Treasure #1 - Priorite Shard

Near the previous collectible you will find a Priorite Shard. It is inside the building.

Chest #1 - Jacket: Wanderer

Cross a small bridge to the other side. You might run into the Commotion Raiders there. Beside them, there is a metal plate that you can push and open another way. This will permit you to leap to a wall close by.

Move as high as possible to move to the following grinding. It will lead you to a spot from where you can land close to the chest.

Treasure #2 - Priorite Shard

Not nowhere near the previous collectible, you will find a gadget opening shortcuts. Above it is a grinding you can climb. Subsequent to scaling, look towards the chest. To one side is a fan and a wall to climb. You want to arrive.

Inevitably, you will get to another grinding, which you should get around. Before it there is a stage you need to reach.

Somewhat further you will go over another wall to climb. Furthermore, you should use the Power to take out the edge.

At the point when you move to the top, you will experience a gathering of opponents. In the wake of overcoming them, you will actually want to pull the component from the wall. Behind it is a passage to another Priorite Shard.

Chest #2 - Legs: Geonosian

In the wake of leaving the small room, go directly to the holder hanging above.

From it, bounce down to the footbridge beneath and afterward go into the dull room in the structure.

Toward the finish of the way you will track down a chest.

Database #2 - Digger Crawler

Get back to the hanging holder and hop onto the wall to climb.

Subsequent to moving for quite a while, you will reach a spot to wall run. When you land, you will see another holder lingering palpably. While standing on it, pull another one.

Star Wars Jedi: Survivor: The Complete Official Guide & Walkthrough

Your next objective is to pull containers on the other hand and thus make a way to the wall to move opposite.

After you reach this objective, continue to go straight until you at last experience a valuable chance to open another shortcut and a gathering of enemies. In the wake of overcoming them, you will actually want to scan the lid of the Digger Crawler.

Treasure #3 - Priorite Shard

Opposite the Digger Crawler is a narrow gap through which you can squeeze. Behind it, in a small square, there is a Priorite Shard.

Treasure #4 - Priorite Shard

Get back to the Digger Crawler and go inside it. A Priorite Shard is there.

Essence

Then you need to go to the rear of the Digger Crawler and use the pulling skill to open the entryway.

In the wake of opening the entryway, you can move higher by getting the grimy edge.

At last, all that remains is to get to the roof of the Digger Crawler, where you track down the Essence. Thanks to it you will get a great deal of XP.

Seed Pod #1 - Bluebell Squish

Return to the meditation point. Then jump down and head straight ahead. From the withered tree you will get seeds.

Seed Pod #2 - Spine Fluff

Go further until you come across a lone small mountain. It contains another Seed Pod. To get there you will need Nekko.

Treasure #5 - Priorite Shard

Not far from the previous collectible, you will find a treasure. However, you need another Nekko to climb to the high ledge.

Seed Pod #3 - Bluebell Squish

After collecting the shard, keep moving forward to the further part of the location. You will eventually find a plant with seeds.

Chest #3 - Head: Geonosian

Get Nekko and stroll back a piece to the put set apart on the guide above. There will be a rope and some walls to run. Thanks to Nekko, you will actually want to reach the zipline.

Then continue pushing ahead using the ropes, wall runs, and leaping off the bars. You will land by a structure on strategic position, which you need to stroll around a little.

Close to the flying animal, you will track down a chest with a cosmetic thing for BD-1.

Chest #4 - Hair: Choppy Forward

Return to the edge where you landed before. You will be able to spot the zipline. Grab onto it and jump to the building opposite.

Run into the building to jump down. You will find a chest there.

Magma Rift Passage

List of secrets in the Magma Rift Passage area

There are **3 collectibles** to find here:

- Databanks: 2
- Treasures: 1

Treasure - Priority Shard

At the large gates serving as a shortcut is a Priorite Shard.

Databank #1 - Caged Nekko

On the lower level there is a cage. Scanning it will give you another databank entry.

Databank #2 - Dark Waters

Star Wars Jedi: Survivor: The Complete Official Guide & Walkthrough

The echo is behind the building nearby. This is a memory of an argument between Turgl and a Bedlam Raider.

Moldy Depths

How to get to Moldy Depths?

You will get there from Harvest Ridge. In the center of the area is a door that is lock with a simple puzzle. All you have to do is first tame the cute creature sitting on the device, and then pull the key to it.

List of secrets in Moldy Depths

There is 1 collectible:

- Treasures: 1

Treasure - Datadisc

Not a long way from the entry you will find a hole through which you can squeeze. From that point forward, you should slide down to the water. Subsequent to landing, go to one side and manage a gathering of enemies on the way. Subsequent to descending a level, another fight awaits you. The treasure is located straightforwardly across from where you landed. This is a Datadisc that you can take to Zee.

How to leave Moldy Depths?

To escape Rotten Depths, you want to mount a Nekko. One is located nearby. Bring it to the entryway set apart in the screenshots above.

Presently you need to go to the other side, get the key and lift the door, then summon Nekko to you.

After everything is finished, you will actually want to leap off its has returned to the high shelf demonstrated in the picture above. Presently you should simply move to the extremely top and thus return to the outside.

Untamed Downs (Part 1)

List of secrets in Untamed Downs

Star Wars Jedi: Survivor: The Complete Official Guide & Walkthrough

There are **38 collectibles** to find here:

- Chests: 6
- Essences: 2
- Databanks: 14
- Treasures: 6
- Seed Pods: 10

Databank #1 - An Ecological Study

Starting from the meditation point, jump down and head to the right, towards the wall. You will find the databank entry.

Treasure #1 - Priorite Shard

The treasure is behind the waterfall opposite the previous collectible.

Databank #2 - Warning Signs

Return to the meditation point and jump to the shelf opposite. After a short walk, you will find the databank entry.

Essence #1

From the location of the previous collectible, head to the left and down. The essence is across from the place where you landed. Beware, however, of three large opponents.

Databank #3 - The Feeding Grounds

There are vines on the surrounding walls. Use them and go up. You will find an echo with a databank entry.

Databank #4 - A Small Mercy

Return to the meditation point (using the nearby vines) and you will be able to go out to the main, central area. There is an echo with a databank entry.

Treasure #2 - Priorite Shard

Opposite the previous collectible is a pile of stones obscuring a Priorite Shard.

Seed Pod #1 - Bluebell Squish

This Seed Pod is relatively close.

Treasure #3 - Priorite Shard

There is a wreck near the above-described plant. Next to it is a Priorite Shard.

Seed Pods #2-4 - Bluebell Squish

From the above-discussed wreck you can leap to the slope close by.

While on it, run ahead and move as high as possible. Then turn right toward the end and head up the slope. There you will track down seven plants with seeds. The first gathering is located in the spot shown in the images above.

Seed Pods #5-8 - Bluebell Squish

Another group is located to the left of the previous one, on the same hill.

Databank #5 - The Ties That Bind

Run towards the white tower and jump down. There is an entrance to a dark cave nearby. In it you will find an echo with a databank entry.

Seed Pod #9 - Spine Fluff

Exit the cave and head left toward the flying creature. Land near the broken bridge. Another plant with seeds is nearby.

Treasure #4 - Priorite Shard

A way prompting the mountain is close by. Snatch and ride a Nekko by following said way. You will reach the stone on which there is a Priorite Shard. You will get to it by leaping off the rear of your mount.

Chest #1 - Material: Hunter

At the bottom is a chest, which you will open by shooting the fuse directly behind it.

Databank #6 - Breaking, Not Entering

Behind the rock where the Priorite Shard was, there is an echo with a databank entry.

Seed Pod #10 - Palm Fruit Shell

The last seed plant in the area is nearby.

Chest #2 - Legs: Swooper

Make a beeline for the right of the closed round entryway and you will find an initial that allows you to see the fuse inside. In the wake of shooting at it, you will actually want to head inside. You'll track down a chest there.

Databank #7 - Bilemaw Burrow

Take the path down (it is near the hole in the wall) and walk towards the cave by the water. Inside it you will find a Bilemaw and a databank entry (this one is located a little deeper).

Databank #8 - Turgle Makes a Deal

At the entrance to the cave is a small chamber on an elevation. You can get to it by jumping off Nekko's back or by using nearby vines.

Chest #3 - Jacket: Mountaineer

From that point, stroll ahead and leap to another edge. You will ultimately reach the chest. To open it you should chase away someone in particular first. Tell her that possession of booty is unlawful.

Chest #4 - Grip: Arakyd Heavy

Leave the cave and head toward the center of the area. You will come across a fuse and a chest located on a rock.

Treasure #5 - Priorite Shard

Standing near the chest, you can see the shelf where the treasure is located. There is a green barrier to the left of it. You need a Nekko to reach it.

Untamed Downs (Part 2)

List of secrets in Untamed Downs

There are **38 collectibles** to find here:

- Chests: 6
- Essences: 2
- Databanks: 14
- Treasures: 6
- Seed Pods: 10

Databank #9 - Technological Betrayal

Head toward the large gate. Behind it you will find an echo with a databank entry. As well as a few mines.

Databank #10 - The Deep Caverns

Overcome the green hindrance close by and afterward head left. Go straight as far as possible until an entryway appears on your ok. A databank section is close to them. Watch out for opponents close by.

Databank #11 - Gift of Fire

Go through the aforementioned door - a legendary enemy awaits behind it. After defeating him, you will be able to enter the room where he was standing. The databank entry is there.

Essence #2

That room also has a valuable essence.

Databank #12 - The Truth

Head to the wall opposite the room you were just in. You should come across the databank.

Databank #13 - Shelter of Last Resort

Get back to the green hindrance and head outside. There is a gadget with mines nearby. Take one with you and bait it by making a beeline for the right until you reach the cavern. It merits going to it first and rout the enemies. From that point forward, you will actually want to use it to destroy the entryway there.

Behind the door is an echo with a databank entry.

Chest #5 - Santari Khri

Near the echo is also a chest with a new lightsaber.

Databank #15 - Mogu Den

Return outside and locate Nekko as soon as possible. Not that a long way from the previous cavern is another one - however this one is very high up, so you need to use your mount.

Hop down while sticking to one side and stroll ahead. You will get to the databank passage soon.

Treasure #6 - Priorite Shard

Use the vines above you to get a level higher. When you are higher up, jump to the shelf behind you. There you will find a Priorite Shard.

Chest #6 - Audio Sensors: Geonosian

Staying on the same level, head straight and go outside. Go right and do a wall run. You will find the last chest in the area and a collectible.

Chamber of Clarity

Chamber of Clarity - list of secrets

There are **7 collectibles** to find here:

- Chests: 1

- Essences: 1

Star Wars Jedi: Survivor: The Complete Official Guide & Walkthrough

- Databanks: 4
- Treasures: 1

Treasure - Datadisc

After leaving the elevator, start by Force Pulling the block in front of you. This will open a pathway. The only Treasure in this region is there.

Databank #1 - Tenacity

From the elevator, run across a few nearby walls. Upstairs, you'll find a scannable echo.

Chest - Unique Non-Metal

From Databank #1 location, go left. Manipulate the blocks so you can go across a chasm to the other side. Continue forward until you find the chest.

Databank #2 - Trials

Hop down to a block tracked down there. Proceed and Power Pull a block somewhat higher up - it has vines on it. Climb the vines and ride the block as far as possible.

You presently need to make two blocks in the following room stand close to one another. With blocks set up this way, you'll have the option to reach the region that was hindered constantly block. The databank section is there.

Databank #3 - Concerted Effort

From Databank #2 area, climb the second block and from it hop toward round entryway.

Behind the entryway, stumble into the wall and go ahead. Another reverberation is here.

Databank #4 - A Candid Moment

Return to the block from which you've jumped to the round door and this time use Force Push to open a neighboring door, also round.

The echo (final one in this zone) is behind the door.

Essence - Perk: Fellowship

From Databank #4 location, Force Push a block nearby and return to the two blocks below. Use Force Pull on both and jump to the second one. It will bring you to the Essence.

Fort Kah'Lin

Fort Kah'Lin - list of secrets

There are **13 collectibles** to find here:

- Chests: 3
- Essences: 1
- Databanks: 5
- Treasures: 1
- Seed Pods: 3

Databank #1 - Bandit Camp

Look for the echo inside the building in the vicinity of the meditation site.

Databank #2 - Victorious Surrender

Head towards one of the doors not a long way from the contemplation point - in the opposite bearing from the stronghold entrance. You will track down a reverberation with a databank passage.

Databank #3 - Past Signs of Life

The echo is another building not far from the meditation point.

Chest #1 - Shirt: Bomber

Head to the hangar which houses a large machine. The chest is inside. Watch out, as there are many enemies in the area. Moreover, another batch of them will emerge from the aforementioned machine (a dropship)

Databank #4 - A House Divided

Leave the storage and head right by following a way driving up. After a short journey, you'll experience a fissure through which you can squeeze through. With the fissure behind you, go left until you reach a small bridge. Behind the bridge there is an inflatable that you can use to reach the upper floor.

Subsequent to arriving on the shelf, go to the structure on the left. The databank passage is there.

Databank #5 - Internal Affairs

In the same building as Databank #4, there is another echo to collect.

Chest #2 - Mountaineer Outfit

Opposite the structure described above, there is another one, with an opening in the entryway. Inside you'll find a NPC with which you really want to converse with open access to the chest. During the conversation, choose the choice saying absence of trust.

Essence

Look around for a nearby bridge, and then go through another bridge. You'll encounter an Essence.

Treasure - Priority Shard

From Essence location, open the nearby shortcut and jump down - you'll will fall into a hole. Defeat the Spawn of Oggdo. Once the area is clear, you can collect the treasure.

Chest #3 - Poncho

In the same area, there is a chest, containing a new appearance item.

Seed Pod #1 - Goldenlight Moss

Return to the ledge above the hole. Look around for climbable vines. Use them to climb down.

After reaching the bottom, approach the edge of the platform. The plant is there.

Seed Pod #2 - Goldenlight Moss

Jump down and proceed to the area where the stream ends. You will find another plant.

Seed Pod #3 - Goldenlight Moss

Keep to the stream but go the opposite direction. After a while you will come across another plant.

Harvest Ridge

Harvest Ridge - list of secrets

There are **23 secrets** to be found:

- Chests: 2
- Essences: 1
- Databanks: 1
- Treasures: 1
- Seed Pods: 18

Seed Pod #1 - Palm Fruit Shell

The first plant can be found at the border where Harvest Ridge connects with Riverbed Watch and Southern Reach regions.

Seed Pod #2 - Palm Fruit Shell

For the second plant, proceed in the direction of a small river. Look near the river bank and left from the small bridge.

Seed Pod #3 - Bluebell Squish

To the right of the aforementioned bridge is another plant, but this time on the inside of the fence.

Seed Pods #4-6 - Bluebell Squish and Palm Fruit Shell

Look for these seeds on a hill nearby.

Seed Pod #7 - Palm Fruit Shell

Slightly farther away from Seed Pods #4-6 there is another plant - look on the border between Harvest Ridge and Untamed Downs.

Seed Pod #8 - Bluebell Squish

Climb upstairs using the shortcut not a long way from Rotten Depths. In the event that you don't have this shortcut opened, there are vines close by that can be accessed by using a Nekko. When you're at the top, go right as far as possible. Another plant is there, right by the wall in the corner. There are some enemies here to overcome as well.

Seed Pod #9 - Palm Fruit Shell

From the large gate, go right and mount one of the Nekkos. With its help, jump over the fence, where the next plant is found.

Seed Pod #10 - Palm Fruit Shell

Mount a Nekko again and this time place yourself at the locked gate of a large building nearby. Jump onto the wall, and from it to a hanging cage. You'll reach an upper floor.

The plant is in the corner, at the fence.

Databank - House on the Range

Turn around and you should see a damaged wall of the building. Rip it out using Force Pull and jump down. You will find an echo with a databank entry.

Chest - Shortpaw's Dance

Return outside and this time move to the roof of the structure. First, you must leap to the enclosure right from the tore out wall, and from it to a bar, lastly reach a climbable wall.

On the roof there is a chest containing a music track.

Essence

Return to the meditation point and this time head down. You'll find an Essence that unlocks a new Perk slot.

Chest #2 - Pants: Wanderer.

Return to the meditation point and grab a hold of a flying creature. Your goal is to reach the area shown in the screenshot above.

The chest is there, containing a new appearance item.

Seed Pod #11 - Palm Fruit Shell

From Chest #2 location, jump to a lower shelf - the plant is there.

Seed Pod #12 - Palm Fruit Shell

From Seed Pod #11 location, turn around and approach the runnable walls. There is another plant in front of them.

Seed Pod #13 - Palm Fruit Shell

Run across the aforementioned walls and go in the direction of the left shelf. You'll encounter a plant.

Treasure #1 - Priorite Shard

At Seed Unit #13 area, there are climbable walls that will assist you with getting upstairs. When you show up to the top, don't do a wall run, however leap to a close by shelf instead. At the shelf, proceed the whole way to the Priorite Shard.

Seed Pods #14-18 - Palm Fruit Shell

From Treasure #1 location, jump to a higher shelf and climb over the fence. The remaining plants are here.

Alignment Control Center

Alignment Control Center - list of secrets

There are **4 collectibles** to find here:

- Chests: 2
- Databanks: 1
- Treasures: 1

Databank #1 - Patience

Starting from the meditation point, instead of going to the elevator, go the opposite way. You'll reach a large hall, inside which is the echo.

Chest #1 - Pommel: Harmony

Get back to the reflection point and this time use the lift. Subsequent to rising up out of the lift, you'll see a room before you. Hop beneath to gather the chest.

Chest #2 - Map Upgrade

At the meditation point itself, there is a device that can be hacked by BD-1, but only if you have all 7 Jedi Meditation Chambers passed/completed.

Treasure - Datadisc

To get the last find, you really want to visit the disaster area in Untamed Downs. From the disaster area, you can leap to a close by slope. Your next waypoint is a white tower seen somewhere far off.

At the point when you are at the tower, move toward the edge shown in the screenshot above. You'll see the Treasure. Hop down and gather it.

Devastated Settlement (Part 1)

List of secrets in the Devastated Settlement

There are **40 collectibles** to find here:

- Chests: 3
- Essences: 5
- Databanks: 15
- Force Tears: 1
- Treasures: 9
- Seed Pods: 7

Seedbag #1 - Crimson Jelly Spire

Jump down to the platform left of the meditation point. The seedbag is near the edge.

Databank #1 - Thermal Vent

Return to the meditation point and get some help from a flying creature to reach the platform in front of you.

Seedbag #2 - Crimson Jelly Spire

Not far from the databank is another Seedbag.

Treasure #1 - Datadisc

Very close by is the Datadisc.

Databank #2 - A Patient Master

Return to the contemplation point and hook onto a close by wall. Then move to the top. From that point, bounce down to the lower stage and take the sphere. Drop it into an opening up on the left wall.

Squeeze through the hole and bounce up from a huge block you've previously pushed under the shelf. You will track down a reverberation with a databank section.

Treasure #2 - Datadisc

Take the sphere and toss it into the speaker. Place a block under where the sphere was previously - strapped in the right wall. Hop up onto the stage and start raising a ruckus around town in the room with the Power. Continue to do this until the speaker moves to one side.

Presently use BD-1's processor and destroy the development on the wall to track down the treasure.

Treasure #3 - Datadisc

Leave the chamber and follow the way up the slope outside. Opposite you is a wall, on which the treasure is - hop on it and slide down it until you reach it. Afterwards, return to solid ground.

Chest #1 - Switch: Harmony

Use a bird to reach the chest visible far away.

It contains a secret. Watch out for nearby enemies.

Seedbag #3 - Crimson Jelly Spire

Near the chest is another seedbag.

Databank #3 - Technological Deficit

Take hold of a flying animal and fly towards the shelf close to a passageway, visible far away.

Hop on the wall close to the passageway and move up. Continue to go head on and you'll have the option to bounce into a small cavern sooner or later. Before that, you'll be gone after by a gathering of enemies, including Goroko.

Inside you'll find a databank reverberation.

Treasure #4 - Datadisc

Use BD-1's grinder to destroy the nearby growth. You'll find the Datadisc next to the orb amplifier.

Essence #1

Take an orb with you and return to the passageway next to the wall you climbed up. Put the orb in the amplifier and you'll unlock the essence behind the newly opened door.

Databank #4 - An Instruction

Return to the amplifier room. The databank echo is in the corner.

Databank #5 - Chamber Mural

Return to the reflection point (using a bird by the destroyed bridge a level higher) and take hold of a flying animal once more. Fly into the fumes from the thermal vent and promptly move to the stage on the right. You'll find a databank section and a gathering of enemies.

Essence #2

Get a close by sphere and follow a close by way profound into the chamber. When there, turn left and toss the sphere onto an opposing stage (where two enemies are).

Run along the wall, get the sphere and move toward the edge. At the base you'll spot an intensifier. Toss the sphere inside - this will help you later.

Presently take the essence saw as adjacent.

Databank #6 - Idle Talk

To the right of the essence you'll find the databank echo.

Treasure #5 - Datadisc

Bounce down - watch out for Goroko - and advance toward the following room, hopping onto a high stage. The treasure is inside a development on the wall. Get it out with BD-1's processor.

Treasure #6 - Datadisc

Return to the previous chamber and you should spot another trapped treasure. Use BD-1's grinder again.

Databank #7 - The Seeds of Concern

Return up and afterward outside, to a flying animal. Head towards the same thermal vent you've used previously. This time you should look into the other vent close by.

In the wake of using it, quickly start moving right. In the wake of landing, head towards the edgewhere you'll find the databank reverberation and a circle enhancer.

Treasure #7 - Datadisc

Get the sphere and enter a chamber through a close by passage. Insert it into the intensifier by and by, this will help you later. Then, haul the block out of an opening in the wall. Bounce into the opening where the block was to track down a Datadisc.

Essence #3 - Perk: Precision

Jump down and head to the rift on the left. After passing through it you'll see a growth covering the essence. Use BD-1's grinder.

Databank #8 - A World Away

To the right of the essence is a databank echo.

Devastated Settlement (Part 2)

List of secrets in the Devastated Settlement

There are **40 collectibles** to find here:

- Chests: 3

- Essences: 5

- Databanks: 15

- Force Tears: 1

- Treasures: 9

- Seed Pods: 7

Databank #9 - Central Manse

Yet again in the wake of gathering the Essence, assume the sphere and position it in the speaker by the edge. In the event that you don't as of now have the pillar focused on the area shown in the screenshot above, do it now, so you don't need to return here.

Get the flying animal and set out toward the smoke on the left, to reach a high shelf with the second contemplation point.

In the wake of landing, continue toward the buildings' left wall. You'll find the databank passage there.

Databank #10 - Training Courtyard

Enter the building and approach the left wall. You should come across the databank.

Databank #11 - Devstated Remains

Use the door opposite to the entrance and go left. Another database entry is there.

Databank #13 - Theses of Yaddle

In the following room there is a reverberation that gathering of is a story occasion - it is impossible to skip it, yet it counts alongside the others. Go into the room left from the table. Another passage is concealed on the bookshelf.

Databank #14 - Cataclysm

Go left to enter the next room. Another entry is here.

Essence #4 - Perk: Marksmanship

Use the Ascension Cable to reach the nearby vines. After reaching a higher floor, go forward and climb the next set of vines. The Essence is there.

Treasure #8 - Datadisc

Grab the flying creature and reach the platform seen in the distance. After landing, be ready to pursue the scavenger droid. Eliminate it as soon as possible.

Seedpods #4-5 - Spine Fluff

There are two plants with seeds in the area.

Chest #2 - Hard Leather

Look for Chest #2 underwater.

Chest #3 - Goatee and Mustache

At the edge, you'll see some vines somewhere far off - you can reach them with Ascension Link.

Move to a higher floor and go quickly right to reach an initial that will lead you to a dim cavern. In front, you'll see a wall - bounce right from it and stumble into the following one. This will give you access to the chest.

Seedpods #6-7 - Crimson Jelly Spire

Go back outside and grab the flying creature to fly in the direction of the beam from the orb amplifier. Reach the area shown in the screenshot above.

The plants are found in this area.

Force Tear - Fractured Punishment

Turn around to see a ruined elevator - the Force Tear is inside. The associated challenge involves defeating enemies in combat. More on the challenge can be viewed on Fractured Punishment page of the guide.

Treasure #9 - Datadisc

Grab the flying creature and fly to the ledge below (the area where you pointed the beam earlier).

Go inside and deal with opponents. Once the area is clear, you're free to collect the datadisc nearby.

Databank #15 - Fallen Padawan

Star Wars Jedi: Survivor: The Complete Official Guide & Walkthrough

Not far from one of the growths there is an echo.

Essence #5 - Perk: Ambidexterity

Use BD-1's processor to destroy a development on the left (looking from the entry). Go in and gather the essence. This is treated as finishing a secret chamber. Assuming that you have all finished yet this one, you can now go to Alignment Control Center and gather the guide redesign.

Rambler's Reach Outpost (Part 1)

List of secrets in the Rambler's Reach Outpost

There are **37 collectibles** to find here:

- Chests: 10
- Essences: 2
- Databanks: 6
- Force Tears: 2
- Treasures: 7
- Seed Pods: 10

Chest #1 - Material: Bomber

Go under your ship's arrival cushion. The entryway close to the reverberation (which doesn't consider a collectible) can be Power Lifted open. You'll track down a chest inside.

Treasure #1 - Priorite Shard

Leave the underside of the arrival cushion by going to one side of the entryway. You'll spot a small Droid holding a Priorite Shard. Dispose of it as soon as possible.

Treasure #2 - Priorite Shard

Nearby, next to the broken bridge, is a second Droid. Don't let it escape.

Star Wars Jedi: Survivor: The Complete Official Guide & Walkthrough

Seed Pod #1 - Bluebell Squish

Nearby, by the fence, you'll find the seed pod.

Seed Pod #2 - Spine Fluff

Nearby, not far away from the fence but near the water, there's another plant.

Seed Pod #3 - Bluebell Squish

A bit further away, by the fence on the other side, there's another seed pod.

Chest #2 - Unique Metal

Mount a Nekko and set out toward the horse shelter entryway from the side of the water. Then bounce up to the window. You'll find a secret entryway you must lift with the right skill. Hop down to track down a chest.

Treasure #3 - Priorite Shard

Go back up but don't jump out of the building just yet. You'll find a Priorite Shard on the wooden footbridge.

Databank #1 - Turgle's Shiny Shell

Leave the structure and make a beeline for the destroyed bridge. To one side of the bridge, by the water, you'll find the databank section.

Chest #3 - Material: Tactical

Head towards Doma's building and jump onto its roof. You can do so from a place not far from the left of the side entrance - use the green canopy.

Inside you'll find clothing.

Seed Pod #4 - Pine Fern

Head to the clearning bordering Hunter's Quarry. You will find another plant.

Databank #2 - The First Move

There are vines close by assuming you push ahead, which you can hook to. In the wake of scaling, go on to the small slope. You will track down a reverberation with a databank section.

Chest #4 - Barrel: Arakyd Heavy

Nearby the aforementioned echo is a chest you can open through Force Lift and Force Slam.

Seed Pod #5 - Pine Fern

Go to the flying animal nearby and use it to fly to the rooftops shown above.

Near Pili there's a withered tree which will give you the seeds.

Chest #5 - Rebel Paint

Climb the vines before you and start moving along them, then drop to the edge inevitably. The chest is by the edge. Destroy it with Power Lift and Power Slam.

Force Tear #1 - Fractured Duality

Get back to the vines and this time climb them the entire way to the top. You'll find a Power Tear. The associated challenge involves overcoming enemies in battle. For additional details, check the Broke Duality page.

Seed Pod #6 - Pine Fern

From the rooftop where the Force Tear was, jump to the hill visible a bit further away.

After a short walk, you'll find the seed plant.

Seed Pod #7 - Pine Fern

To the right of the above-described plant there is another.

Seed Pod #8 - Pine Fern

Again to the right, though this time a level below, there's another plant.

Seed Pod #9-10 - Pine Fern

Star Wars Jedi: Survivor: The Complete Official Guide & Walkthrough

On the hill in front of you are the last two plants in the area.

Chest #6 - Pommel: Edgehawk

Near the plants is a chest holding a saber pommel.

Databank #3 - Relter Egg

Across from the chest is a databank entry.

Rambler's Reach Outpost (Part 2)

List of secrets in the Rambler's Reach Outpost

There are **37 collectibles** to find here:

- Chests: 10
- Essences: 2
- Databanks: 6
- Force Tears: 2
- Treasures: 7
- Seed Pods: 10

Chest #7 - Map Upgrade: Seed Pods

Go to Pili and plant ten unique plants in the close by garden. Presently you must sit tight for them to sprout - you can check how long it takes while dealing with the nursery.

Return when they're prepared and plant another ten unique plants. You'll be compensated with a guide overhaul.

Treasure #4 - Priorite Shard

Climb the close by vines to the exceptionally top. There, get a flying animal and fly towards the structure. You must arrive on the highest part.

You will track down a Priorite Shard.

Databank #4 - Forever Curious

Get back to the region where the most buildings are and make a beeline for the structure neighboring the Hunter's Quarry region. You'll find an entryway covered with cables. Cut them and have BD-1 hack it open.

Inside you'll find a databank section.

Databank #5 - Obsession

You'll find another entry in the same room.

Databank #6 - Soont Madas

To get the next entry you must talk to the character in the building. Say you're a friend. This will open a passage to the bottom.

You'll find an echo with a databank entry.

Essence #1

The essence is in the same room.

Treasure #5 - Datadisc

You must have enrolled Jawa to see as the following collectible. You can do as such at the backhoe in the Former Settlement. Then, you must converse with the Prospector in the spot presented previously.

Assuming you've selected Jawa, go to the structure presented previously. You will track down a treasure.

Treasure #6 - Datadisc

There's another treasure in the opposite building.

Chest #7 - Blaster: Swoop

In the same building there's a fuse you must use the BD-1 Electro Dart on. This will openthe side door. You'll find a chest holding a new Blaster.

Essence #2

Star Wars Jedi: Survivor: The Complete Official Guide & Walkthrough

Move to the roof of the structure where you've tracked down the new weapon - use the boxes close to the exit. When there, eliminate the key from the gadget and move it to the indistinguishable gadget on the contiguous roof. You'll open the entryway in the second structure.

Inside you'll track down the Essence.

Chest #8 - Max Stims Increase

To reach the following chest, you must purchase the Mysterious Keycode from Doma. It costs 10 Priorite Shards.

Having gotten it, you can now pass through a close by entryway. In the recently opened room you'll find an enormous chest holding a Stim redesign.

Force Tear #2 - Fractured History

For the following collectible you must have crushed the unbelievable foe in Stronghold Kah'linand gathered essence from a frog you'll see as neighboring. Then, in Doma's ship, gather essence once more. This will open a Tear. For additional details, check the Cracked History page.

Chest #9 - Jacket: Duelist

To access the following chest, you must have enlisted T-1N8 - tracked down before the entry to Phon'qi Caverns. Assuming that you've done so as of now, you'll find her in the spot presented previously.

Converse with her and you'll have the option to enter the close by building. There's a chest inside.

Treasure #7 - Priorite Shard

To obtain the last treasure nearby, you must trust that a purple Nekko will show up in the enclosure (you can over and over rest at the reflection point until it does).

After you track down it, lead it to the animal dwellingplace. Leave it at the demonstrated spot and rest at a contemplation point. Return here to get the Priorite Shard.

Jedha

Monastery Walls on Jedha

Monastery Walls - list of secrets

There are 19 collectibles to find in Monastery Walls:

- Chests: 6
- Essences: 2
- Databanks: 3
- Force Tear: 1
- Treasure: 7

Databank #1 - Pilgrims, Lost

Starting from the meditation point, head to the leftmost part of the ruins. The secret is in an area where you encounter a few smaller monsters.

Treasure #1

This Jedha Scroll is on the ground next to the previous (Databank #1) collectible.

Force Tear #1 - Fractured Tradition

You want to reach the left piece of the ruins and get the hitch while sliding down a steep slope. You'll end up in the space shown in screenshot 1, from where you can bounce and follow a way spread out by columns.

At last, Cal reaches the upper shelf set apart in screenshot 1 and that is where the tear is located.

Chest #1

The chest is on the same shelf as the previously mentioned Force Tear. You'll find an appearance item inside.

Chest #2

From the area where you've found the previous chest, you really want to do an upward run. This will permit you to access the upper piece of the ruins where the new compartment is found. Inside, you'll track down an apperance thing.

Treasure #2

Don't leave the area yet - a Jedha Scroll is on the ground in the same location.

Treasure #3

After getting the scroll (previous subsection) jump to a nearby shelf. You'll find another Jedha Scroll there.

Chest #3

Search for this chest on a more significant level in the leftmost piece of the ruins. To arrive, you'll have to do a wall run. Plunder it to get an appearance thing for BD-1.

Databank #2 - Prayer Wheel

Start at the meditation point and slide down the slope on the right. Simply let BD-1 scan the object.

Treasure #4

This Jedha Scroll is on the ground in the central part of the ruins - the same area where you encounter a group of enemies.

Chest #4

The chest is in the right piece of the ruins - the same where you experience a stormtrooper unit. It contains an appearance thing for BD-1.

Databank #3 - Communal Space

You must reach the rightmost region of the ruins - en route, watch out for a burrowing monster. In the wake of reaching the area and overcoming a gathering of smaller creatures, BD-1 can scan the region.

Treasure #5

This Jedha Scroll is in the rightmost region of the ruins not a long way from the previously mentioned Databank. Close to the collectible, you can also spread out the rope thus opening a shortcut.

Chest #5

First you really want to reach the top walls and the way to them leads through the left region of the ruins.

Follow the walls until you reach a bronze chest (screenshot 1). Inside, you'll track down a blaster - Skeleton Key.

Treasure #6

This Jedha Scroll is before the right area of the ruins. Look for a small niche near the wall.

Chest #6

The chest is on a higher shelf in the central area of the ruins. Loot it to receive an appearance item for BD-1.

Essence #1

You want to reach the back region of the ruins and accessing this area is possible after a series of wall runs. The first wall is shown in screenshot 1 (you'll perceive that you can do a wall run thanks to white tone) and you want to keep going through further walls. At long last, you'll reach a small room containing the Essence, which extends your wellbeing bar.

Essence #2

In the wake of getting the first Essence, move to the highest point of one of the structures that had walls suitable for wall running on their sides. You must reach the remote walls set apart in screenshot 1. Hop from that spot to a dim region underneath and you'll find the Essence, which gives a XP boost.

Treasure #7

This Jedha Scroll is in the same area as Essence #2 from the previous subsection.

Penitent Chambers

Penitent Chambers - list of secrets

There are **5 collectibles** to find here:

- Chests: 2
- Essences: 1
- Treasures: 2

Treasure #1

Jedha Scroll #1 is found in the ruins encountered soon after meeting Merrin for the first time and climbing to an upper shelf with her help.

Chest #1

In the ruins, you can run up a vertical wall and reach an upper shelf. There is a chest there, containing an appearance item.

Essence #1

Further en route, you'll experience a possibility to bounce up to an intelligent hitchat a wall adjoining the primary way. From that point, you can go through adjacent walls.

Reach the spot by leaping off an upward wall. The Essence is on an upper shelf and getting it is compensated with a XP boost.

Treasure #2

Start where you've found Essence #1, pivot and go ahead along the upper ruins. En route you can alternatively open 2 shortcuts driving back to the lower part of the ruins.

Hop down to the lower corridor. There you'll experience a stormtrooper and a scavenger droid that has to be removed from commission for example by making a lightsaber toss. Crushed scavenger leaves another Jedha Scroll.

Chest #2

The chest is in the same area as the encountered scavenger droid. Loot it to receive an appearance item for BD-1.

Halls of Ranvell

Halls of Ranvell - secrets

There are 10 collectibles:

- Chests: 2
- Essences: 2
- Databanks: 4
- Treasures: 2

Databank #1 - Pilgrims, Attacked

This reverberation is found just after a scene where Cal and Merrin spot a Spamel in a distance. This is close to a contemplation point.

Treasure #1

Treasure #1 is found not far from the previous (Databank #1) collectible. You can find it next to a door that is initially locked (it is opened later on from the other side).

Essence #1

Close to the contemplation point, you can bounce up to a rough shelf, and from that point you can go up climbable walls (screenshot 1). Essence #1 is at the exceptionally top and when gotten gives a XP boost.

Chest #1

Soon subsequent to overcoming a bigger gathering of stormtroopers you will wind up close to several levels of ruins. You must reach the floor with the chest. It contains an appearance thing for Cal.

Databank #2 - Ancient Ruins

You will find this collectible during your path through the ruins, soon after the section where you grab the ceiling.

Treasure #2

This Jedha Scroll is above 2 walls that you can bounce off back and forth. Reach the upper area with this method.

Databank #3 - Scorch Marks

Prior to entering the region with the workbench, look at the metal way driving down. There will be some small monsters to overcome en route. Reach the flip side of the way and let BD-1 scan the region.

Essence #2

In the specific place where the previous collectible (Databank #3) was, search for a spot that you can leap to - the screenshot shows it. You'll find an Essence there which guarantees a XP boost when gotten.

Chest #2

Reach the region in ruins with a workbench and a gathering of stormtroopers (something like one of them will have a shield). When the foe is disposed off, search for a chest that contains an appearance thing for BD-1.

Databank #4 - Ancient Wars

Simply scan the mural (in the same room as the previous find).

Divine Oasis

Divine Oasis - list of secrets

There are **3 collectibles** to find here:

- Databanks: 1

- Treasures: 2

Databank #1 - Pilgrims, Saved

Look for a tent in the area with spamels.

Treasure #1

A Jedha Scroll is also at the tent.

Treasure #2

Look for this one on a higher shelf. You have to jump from a spamel (screenshot 1) to reach this area. In the same area there is also a unlockable shortcut.

Sheltered Hollow

Sheltered Hollow - list of secrets

There are 2 collectibles to find here:

- Chests: 1
- Treasures: 1

Chest #1 - Stim Canister

The yellow chest with the Stim Canister is not far from the encampment where Cal and Merrin take shelter from the sandstorm.

Treasure #1

On further visits to Sheltered Empty you can experience a scavenger droid there. Make up for lost time to it and kill it for example with a lightsaber toss. The droid will leave a treasure - a Jedha Scroll.

Desert Passages

Desert Passages - list of secrets

There are 3 collectibles to find here:

- Chest: 2
- Databank: 1

Chest #1

The chest is in a side room that contains a speeder bike. Loot it to receive the Solar paint job for BD-1.

Databank #1 - The Witch

This echo is in a circular room near the exit from Cere.

Chest #2

In the main room, use Force Push on the orbs so they stop in locations shown in the screenshot. This will open a door on the lowest level.

Look there for a chest. The chest contains a lightsaber part.

Trailhead Pantheon

Trailhead Pantheon (Jedha) - list of secrets

There are 9 collectibles:

- Chest: 2
- Databanks: 4
- Treasure: 3

Databank #1 - The Path

Scan the stone tablet encountered right after reaching this region for the first time.

Chest #1

Chest #1 is in a side corridor close to the roundabout lobby. Move the block with Power and the collectible will be uncovered. Inside, you'll find a lightsaber apperance thing.

Databank #2 - Ancient Crypt

The area to scan is in the titular ancient crypt which can be accessed after climbing a stony block.

Treasure #1

This Jedha Scroll is in the same crypt as the previous (Databank #2) collectible.

Treasure #2

This Jedha Scroll is in ruins that are at first inaccessible. You will access this area in the course of the primary story in the wake of finishing a more drawn out climb and some leaping to upper ledges.

Databank #3 - Map of Pilgrim's Path

The large map is in the same building in the ruins as the previous (Treasure #2) collectible.

Treasure #3

Treasure #3 is found in an area which you'll access after completing a series of wall runs. It is not far from the Crypt of Uhrma meditation point.

Databank #4 - Meditation Room

This titular Meditation Room is circular and you'll visit it shortly after passing through the Crypt of Uhrma meditation point.

Chest #2

Stay where you've found Databank #4 and perform a long wall run to reach a chest marked in screenshot 1. Inside the chest you'll find a Jedi outfit for Cal.

Blustery Mesa

List of secrets to be found in Blustery Mesa

There are 7 collectibles to find here:

- Chest: 1

- Databanks: 2

- Force Tear: 1

- Treasures: 3

Chest #1

The chest can be found just after reaching the Blustery Mesa from the Trailhead Pantheon. Inside, you'll find a lightsaber apperance item.

Databank #1 - Ghost or Guardian

After completing the sequence of sliding down a slippery slope and defeating a group of small monsters, you will find the echo.

Databank #2 - Catacombs of the Weary

The area to be scanned is next to the main entrance to Crypt of Uhrma.

Treasure #1

The Jedha scroll is on one of the upper ledges, close to the lift going to Grave of Uhrma and the vantage point from which you can see the Old Bridge.

Treasure #2

You must approach the passage to the adjoining Trailhead Pantheon (you can open a shortcut). Cal can make a wall run here. Make a point to reach the lower region with the scavenger droid. Use a fast assault or a lightsaber toss. The crushed droid drop a Jedha scroll.

Force Tear #1 - Fractured Dexterity

After acquiring the above secret, find a green gate in the lower corridors that requires the Merrin's Charm. After getting past the gate, you'll find yourself in a crypt with the Tear. There is a battle challenge to be completed here.

Treasure #3

Start close to the lift going to Sepulcher of Uhrma. The spot in the screenshot 1 presents the solution to the puzzle inside the grave, yet you can also leap to this rock shelf. In the spot set apart in the screenshot you can find a Jedha Scroll.

Crypt of Uhrma

Crypt of Uhrma - list of secrets

There are 5 collectibles to find here:

- Chests: 1

- Essences: 1

- Databanks: 2

- Treasures: 1

Databank #1 - Companions of the Caretakers

You have to scan the skeletons in the initial area of the crypt.

Treasure #1

Treasure #1 (Jedha Scroll) is in the initial area of the crypt.

Chest #1 - Stim Canister

To access the Stim Canister, you need to open an enormous entryway in the grave and the associated puzzle is described exhaustively on a committed page (Sepulcher of Uhrma on Jedha).

When that is far removed, search for an enormous yellow chest. Inside, you'll track down a Stim Canister that increases your recuperating capabilities by 1.

Databank #2 - Voices of the Wind

You can find this echo in the same area of the crypt as the aforementioned Stim Canister.

Essence #1

Subsequent to opening the huge entryway in the Grave, use Power Pull to tear out a mesh from screenshot 1.

You will reach a region with a fishery and a shortcut to Trailhead Pantheon. Proceed with the primary passage to reach a green entryway (screenshot 2). You can move beyond it in the wake of opening Merrin's Appeal in the fundamental story.

Squeeze between the rocks. Here you need to overcome a discretionary boss - Sutaban Alpha. In the wake of overcoming the beast, look at her nest to find an Essence that awards the Speculator perk - it will increase the XP gain, yet subsequent to passing on, Cal can't recover his lost experience points.

Singing Ruins

Singing Ruins - list of secrets

There are **2 collectibles** to find here:

- Databanks: 1
- Treasures: 1

Databank #1 - Trespassers of the Storm

The sought echo is by the skeleton in the dark part of the ruins.

Treasure #1

This Jedha Scroll is found in the ruins soon in the wake of squeezing through the rocks. Use your lightsaber to light the way and locate the secret all the more easily.

Sepulcher Pass

Sepulcher Pass - list of secrets

There is only 1 collectible to be found here:

- Treasures: 1

Treasure #1

This sole Jedha Scroll can be easily found on your first visit to Sepulcher Pass for example while escaping with Merrin not long in the wake of getting the appeal used to pass green gates.

The secret is tracked down on the ground close to the reflection point.

Veiled Hangar

Veiled Hangar - list of secrets

There are 3 collectiblesto find here:

- Chest: 2
- Databank: 1

Chest #1

The chest is on the upper level (to get there, use the elevator near Mantis), at the rocks. When looted, it contains an appearance item for Cal.

Databank #1 - The Master's Arrival

The echo is at the end of the path on the upper level of the hangar.

Chest #2

Look for it next to the passageway connecting Veiled Hangar and The Archive. Inside, you'll find Cere Jund's lightsaber.

The Archive

The Archive - list of secrets

There are 11 collectibles:

- Chest: 2
- Essences: 2
- Databanks: 2

- Treasure: 5

Treasure #1

This Jedha Scroll is in a side area on the ground floor which is accessed by using a narrow passage leading between the walls.

Databank #1 - Old Connections, New Paths

This Databank is on the ground floor in the back area of The Archive, not far from Sister Taske's shop.

Databank #2 - A New Path

In one of the corners in the back area of The Archive.

Essence #1

To have the option to access this find, you really want to have redesigned Ascension Rope, which is gotten with sufficient progress in the principal storyline. In the back region of The File, connect yourself to the inflatable from screenshot 1. The Essence is on the upper shelf, and it awards a XP boost.

Chest #1

In the side region of The File, find where you can squeeze through - it will lead you to a green entryway (screenshot 1). Assuming you have Merrin's Appeal, simply pass to the other side and plunder the chest. Inside, you'll find a lightsaber apperance thing.

Treasure #2

Treasure #2 (Jedha Scroll) can be found once the upper area of The Archive has been unlocked. Again, you can attach yourself to the balloon by using upgraded Ascension Rope.

Treasure #3

From the location of the previous collectible, reach the neighboring upper shelf. You'll find a Jedha Scroll in the area shown in the screenshot above.

Essence #2

Stay on the upper shelves of The Archive. Look around them to find an Essence which extends the Force bar.

Chest #2

Another collectible found on upper shelves of The Document - to have the option to access this one, you want to open BD-1 Electro Dart (enough progress in the primary story).

Reach the locked chest (screenshot 1). To gain admittance, you really want to use the electro dart on a blue fuse taken cover behind the wall and afterward rapidly plunder the chest. The chest contains a lightsaber apperance thing.

Treasure #4

This Jedha Scroll is another collectible found on the upper shelves of The Archive.

Treasure #5

Treasure #5 (Jedha Scroll) is not far from Sister Taske's store in the back area of The Archive.

Path of Persistence

Path of Persistence - list of secrets

There are 5 collectiblesto find here:

- Chests: 1
- Essences: 1
- Databanks: 2
- Treasures: 1

Databank #1 - Cordova's Travels on Jedha I

You can easily find this one right after entering the ruins and reaching a side shelf.

Databank #2 - Cordova's Wonder

This echo is found on the top level of the ruins, next to a ball track used in the puzzle.

Chest #1

This chest is found on the side shelf in the ruins. Loot it to receive a paint job for BD-1 - Industrial.

Essence #1

First you need to solve the Way of Persistence puzzle - we described it exhaustively in Puzzles section of the aide. Subsequent to conveying the circle to the top and pushing it with Power, a side reserve containing the Essence will open. Take it to open another Advantage slot.

Treasure #1

This Jedha Scroll is one of the lower shelves in the ruins, next to a place where you can surprise attack a sitting stormtrooper.

Path of Restoration

List of secrets to be found on the Path of Restoration

There are 5 collectiblesto find here:

- Chests: 1
- Essences: 1
- Databanks: 3

Databank #1 - Cordova's Travels on Jedha II

The region to be scanned is under one of the paths to move the orbs. You can arrive during the underlying phase of the ruins' investigation.

Databank #2 - A Voice to the Past

You will find the echo after making a run along the wall and finding yourself next to the orb, which can be pushed using the Force.

Chest #1

In the wake of tracking down the previous secret, move up to the edge with stormtroopers and a rope. After the battles, track down the chest with Cal's clothing thing.

Databank #3 - A Master's Realization

This echo is found on the top level of the ruins, next to a ball track used in the puzzle.

Essence #1

You have to solve the riddle of the Path of Restoration - we described it in the chapter Riddles. After delivering the orb to the top and pushing it with Force, a side cache containing the Essence will unlock. Take it to unlock a new Perk slot.

Path of Conviction

List of secrets to be found on the Path of Conviction

There are 4 collectiblesto find in Sheltered Hollow region of Jedha:

- Chests: 1
- Essences: 1
- Databanks: 1
- Treasures: 1

Databank #1 - Digging Deeper

This echo is found on the top level of the ruins, next to a ball track used in the puzzle.

Essence #1

You need to solve the conundrum of the Way of Conviction - we described it in the section Riddles. In the wake of conveying the sphere to the top and pushing it with Power, a side store containing the Essence will open. Take it to open another Advantage slot.

Chest #1

The chest is on the lower level of the ruins and is guarded by a droid. In the container you will find BD-1 materials.

Treasure #1

The Jedha Scroll is hidden in the vase in screenshot 1 - you must break it. This is an area of ruins immediately adjacent to the precipice.

Wayfinder's Tomb

List of secrets to be found in Wayfinder's Tomb

There are 5 collectiblesto find here:

- Chests: 2

- Databanks: 2

- Treasures: 1

Databank #1 - Cordova's Travels on Jedha IV

You must trip the slope contiguous the Parched Flats area. Scan the closed trapdoor on top of the burial chamber.

We described the conundrum of opening the burial chamber on a separate page named Wayfinder's Burial place. Accessing it is expected to acquire the 3 other secrets described beneath.

Databank #2 - The Final Lesson

You will find the echo inside the tomb.

Chest #1 - Map upgrade: Treasures

The terminal to be hacked by BD-1 is inside the burial place.

This is a one of a kind secret, because you can get a treasure map. Starting here on, all undiscovered treasures will show up on the holographic guide.

We have described other realistic treasure maps on a separate page named Guide Upgrades.

Chest #2

The chest is another secret to be found inside the tomb. It contains Eno Cordova's lightsaber.

Treasure #1

This secret is located on the burial chamber, especially not inside it. You need to sneak up on the scavenger droid portrayed in the screenshot 1 and toss a lightsaber at it. On the off chance that the machine escapes and burrows underground, use fast travel to reload the guide and attempt once more.

The droid will drop a Jedha scroll.

Timeworn Bridge

List of secrets to be found in Timeworn Bridge

There are **4 collectibles** to find in Sheltered Hollow region of Jedha:

- Chests: 1
- Force Tear: 1
- Treasures: 2

Treasure #1

You will find the Jedha scroll near the meditation point, just after opening the passage with the Force.

Treasure #2

You will find the Jedha scroll after defeating a group of enemies, using a grappling hook and making a wall run.

Force Tear #1 - Fractured Cunning

Start at the contemplation point and follow the fundamental climbing way. En route, you should experience a green door (to have the option to get to the other side of it, you really want to progress in the fundamental story enough to get Merrin's Appeal). The Tear is on the other side of a laser door. There is a battle challenge associated with it using the Blaster stance in fight.

Chest #1

The secret is in the bridge and at first you can't reach it.

Get back to the bridge from the Sanctuary Restored (two limited passages between rocks). You can get the rope from screenshot 1 and bounce with it to the remote climbing wall on the bridge. Rout the stormtroopers and take a long leap toward the second climbing wall from screenshot 2.

You will reach where you can cut the ropeand make a shortcut. Get the rope and reach the contiguous piece of the bridge. On the left is the chest set apart in the screenshot 1. Inside, you will track down a hardware appearance thing.

Arid Flats

List of secrets to be found in Arid Flats

There are 24 collectiblesto find in Sheltered Hollow region of Jedha:

- Chests: 4

- Essences: 3

- Databanks: 8

- Treasures: 9

Databank #1 - Foundation

You will find the echo at the entrance to the Cere base, that is, next to the Desert Passages region.

Databank #2 - The Beasts of Jedha

You will find the echo by the skeleton in the desert, near the Anachoret Base meditation point.

Chest #1

The chest is next to the Arid Flats meditation point. You'll find an appearance item inside.

Databank #3 - Debt

Scan the corpse of a stormtrooper by the rocks.

Databank #4 - The Desert Ghost

Another dead stormtrooper can be found on the rocks near the meditation point and where Skoova fishes.

Databank #5 - Cordova's Travels on Jedha

The place to scan is on the border with the Path of Conviction ruins.

Treasure #1

The Jedha scroll is in the possession of a scavenger droid a short distance from the Wayfinder's Burial chamber. You need to get him and search the remains of the machine.

Databank #6 - A Warning

The echo is next to one of the meditation points.

Databank #7 - Cere's Journey

You can find the echo at the base of the hill, at the top of which is the entrance to the Wayfinder's Tomb.

Chest #2

The chest is on a high section of the ruins. You must start at the Wayfinder's Burial chamber and have the updated grappling rope from the fundamental storyline opened. Cal can launch toward the ruins presented in the screenshot. There are a yellow relter and a compartment concealing an appearance thing.

Essence #1

This can be tracked down in a higher section of the ruins. You must start at the Wayfinder's Burial chamber and make a beeline for the edge set apart in screenshot 1. Use twofold jumps followed by a dash en route. The essence you secure extends Cal's wellbeing bar.

Treasure #2

You will find the Jedha scroll at the base of the ruins, on top of which was the essence described above.

Treasure #3

The Jedha scroll is on the ruins, which you can reach from the Wayfinder's Burial chamber. You must use the better inflatable catching snare and land on the stone shelf set apart in the screenshot 1.

Essence #2

In the wake of securing the treasure from the previous subsection, keep reaching all the more high ledges from the area. Reach the edge shown in the screenshot. You can take a jump from it toward the climbing wall.

You will get to a shelf with a relter and a cordial NPC. Converse with this person and use mind control (the decision of discourse choice does not make any difference). You will open an entryway, behind which is an essence that grants you XP.

Treasure #4

The Jedha scroll is on a lower shelf in the same ruins where you found the essence described above.

Treasure #5

Reach the base of the ruins where you got the previous 3 secrets. There is a scavenger droid nearby - you must toss your lightsaber at it or get up to speed to it and play out a skirmish sword assault. You'll obtain a Jedha Scroll.

Treasure #6

The Jedha scroll is hidden in a cave occupied by monsters. The entrance to it is shown in the screenshot 1.

Essence #3

The essence is in the same cave as the treasure described above. It grants you XP.

Databank #8 - The Pilgrims of Jedha

You will find the echo in the same cave where the 2 previous secrets were located.

Chest #3

The chest is on a small hill adjacent to the monster cave where you found the previous 3 secrets. The container conceals a clothing item.

Treasure #7

You have to get the scavenger droid, which is hiding near the shipwreck and the meditation point. Hit it with a lightsaber, and the droid will drop a Jedha scroll.

Treasure #8

The Jedha scroll is on a high stone edge close to the contemplation point and where Skoova fishes. You must have a redesigned catching snare opened, take hold of the inflatable and launch yourself from it toward the shelf with the secret.

Treasure #9

Not a long way from where the treasure from the previous subsection was gotten is the sanctuary of a skriton. Rout the scaled down boss. You want to use the Power lift at the spot in screenshot 1 subsequent to opening this skill in the principal storyline. With this, a Jedha Scroll will show up.

Chest #4

After getting the previous secret, climb to a higher ledge to get to a chest. You'll find an appearance item inside.

Desert Ridge

List of secrets of the Desert Ridge region

There are **9 collectibles** to find here:

- Chests: 4

- Essences: 1

- Databanks: 2

- Force Tear: 1

- Treasures: 1

Essence #1

The essence is close to the nest of the brilliant Skriton - a discretionary boss from Jedha. You will acquire an advantage that allows you to overlook 1 foe assault while charging a blaster shot.

Force Tear #1 - Fractured Resolve #2

You can reach the rift by penetrating the green gate hidden in the rocks (screenshot 1) and this is possible after unlocking Merrin's Charm in the main storyline. There will be a challenge to pass - completing an obstacle course.

Chest #1

The chest is right next to the meditation point. Loot it to receive an appearance item for BD-1.

Databank #1 - Jedha Politics

You will also find the echo in the small ruins next to the meditation point.

Chest #2

The chest is toward the finish of the way prompting the cliff, close to where the rope is hung up, and a shortcut is made. The compartment contains an appearance thing.

Databank #2 - Pilgrimage

Echo is in the cave. The entrance to it is shown in the screenshot 1. You have to tear it down using the Force. There are also several small monsters to eliminate.

Chest #3

The chest is on the ledge next to the place where you can create a shortcut by cutting the rope. The chest contains a piece of music for Pyloon's Saloon.

Treasure #1

Start where you tracked down the chest - the previous secret. You need to run along the wall and leap to the climbing wall. The secret has to be gotten while slowly sliding down an upward wall.

Chest #4

Reaching the last container is risky, as it is on a seemingly inaccessible high edge - as shown in the screenshot. It is close to the contemplation point and the region is watched by AT-STs, among others. You can't do customary climbing because there are no hooks and the ledges are excessively high.

You need to move to the highest point of the surrounding ruins - this is a district called the Way of Conviction.

Find the yellow relter in the screenshot 1. You need to get the bird and soar towards the edge from the adjoining locale.

In the wake of arriving on a high stone shelf, reach the chest you are searching for. Inside, you'll find a lightsaber apperance thing.

Narkis Highlands

List of secrets to be found across Narkis Highlands

There are **5 collectibles** to find here:

- Chests: 2
- Essences: 2
- Treasures: 1

Chest #1

Reach the area with a stone block that can be moved. It must be in a drawn out position. This will permit you to look at the side region set apart in the screenshot 1. The chest contains the BD-1 appearance thing.

Chest #2

Reach the skriton's lair. After defeating the mini-boss, climb to a higher ledge and run on the wall. You will reach a chest with BD-1 appearance items.

Essence #1

Close to the contemplation point from the adjoining Bone-dry Flats, you can hang 2 ropes. Stand by the one shown in the screenshot and leap to the climbing walls. You must take hold of the bars and move to one side, then take hold of the roof.

In the long run you will reach an isolated stone edge with an essence. It grants you XP.

Treasure #1

Where the skriton is experienced, Cal can take hold of the inflatable in the screenshot 1 - you first need to open the redesigned catching snare in the principal storyline. Launch yourself towards the running wall and reach the edge with the Jedha scroll.

Essence #2

From where you found the previous secret, do a wall run. This will enable the hero to reach the ledge with the relter and the second essence allocating XP.

Whistling Drop

List of secrets at the Whistling Drop

There are **5 collectibles** to find here:

- Chests: 2
- Databanks: 2
- Treasures: 1

Databank #1 - One Journey Ends

You will find the echo in front of the green gate, near the meditation point.

Treasure #1

The Jedha scroll is on a circular arena where a large group of stormtroopers originally stayed. Cal arrives at this place after a longer climb.

Chest #1

The chest is concealed under a consuming wreck where you experience a Skriton and supreme officers. The compartment conceals a component of the presence of Cal's hardware.

Databank #2 - Onwards, Traveller

You have to scan the inscriptions on the wall by the path running above the Trailhead Pantheon. In the same location, you can also unlock a shortcut to the said region.

Chest #2

Next to the meditation point is the path to the green gate and you can return to it after unlocking 2 in the storyline. There is an element of equipment appearance in the chest.

Sanctuary Temple

List of secrets to be found at Sanctuary Temple

There are 6 collectiblesto find here:

- Essence: 1
- Databanks: 3
- Treasures: 2

Treasure #1

The Jedha scroll lies on the ground near the main entrance to the ruins from the main storyline.

Databank #1 - The Destination and the Beginning

You can scan the mural right after squeezing between the rocks at the main entrance to the ruins and receiving the task of finding Brother Armias.

Databank #2 - Sanctuary Revived

The reverberation by the jugs is to be tracked down shortly after the painting from the previous secret. This takes place shortly prior to reaching the contemplation point.

Database #3 - Underground sewers

The echo is to be found in one of the side corridors adjacent to the main hall of the temple.

Treasure #2

In the main hall of the temple, you need to get to a side room with a workbench and a Jedha Scroll.

Essence #1

In the same location where you found the previous secret, you will see a green gate. Cal can only penetrate it after unlocking Merrin's Charm. Essence allocates XP.

Buried Refuge

List of secrets at Buried Refuge

There are **6 collectibles** to find here:

- Chest: 1
- Databanks: 3
- Treasures: 2

Chest #1

Just before you swim to the room with the locked gate, you must find a chest in the underwater tunnel. Loot it to receive an appearance item for BD-1.

Treasure #1

The Jedha Scrollis in the same room where you solve the mandatory puzzle of opening the gate in the Buried Refuge.

Databank #1 - Hidden Path, Exposed

You can scan the skeletons shortly after solving the puzzle of opening the big gate.

Databank #2 - Temple Evacuation

You will find the echo in the same corridor as the previous secret.

Databank #3 - A Noble Deed

The secret is in the round room, which you will reach shortly after completing the puzzle of opening the gate. This is an important find linked to Brother Armias.

Treasure #2

The Jedha scroll is in the same room as the previous secret.

Shattered Moon

Cargo Loading Deck

List of secrets in the Cargo Loading Deck

There is 1 collectible:

- Treasures: 1

Treasure #1

You can find the datadisk next to Mantis, which is the landing site where the exploration of the Shattered Moon begins.

Automated Forge

List of secrets to be found in Automated Forge

There are **15 collectibles** to find here:

- Chests: 3
- Essences: 2
- Databanks: 4
- Force Tear: 1
- Treasures: 5

Databank #1 - The Unconvinced

The echo is at the terminal found just after reaching the forge for the first time.

Databank #2 - In the Name of Science

The Echo is in the control room near the meditation point.

Databank #3 - Droid Recharging Station

You can scan the station in a rectangular room, where you had to defeat a large group of droids and Bedlam Raiders.

Treasure #1

After getting the previous secret, unlock the exit from the station room and turn left. The datadisk is hidden on the right side next to the crates.

Chest #1

Stay where you saw as the previous secret. At the spot shown in the screenshot, make a run along the walls and you will reach the chest visible somewhere far off. The chest hides weapons material for changing the presence of the hardware.

Chest #2

The chest is in the room where you defeat the Magnaguard boss in the storyline. After the duel, take the equipment appearance item from the container.

Databank #4 - Monitoring Station

You can reach the station to be scanned from the side of the edge, where shortcuts are opened (hanging ropes). At the spot shown in the screenshot 1, you must use the stick and run right when the hot steam trap is switched off.

Treasure #2

The datadisk is in a dark corner in the same room where the station from the previous secret was.

Force Tear #1 - Fractured Endurance

You will find the tear in the same room as the 2 previous secrets. You must complete the combat challenge of defeating 150 battle droids.

Chest #3

Close to the contemplation point, you can bounce on small ledges with hot steam - the first one is shown in the screenshot 1. Trust that the steam will switch off. Hop onto the edge with a box that contains a lightsaber appearance thing.

Essence #1

Star Wars Jedi: Survivor: The Complete Official Guide & Walkthrough

Close to the reflection point, you can stroll on yellow pipes. Position yourself at the spot shown in the screenshot 1 and make a run along the wall toward the essence visible somewhere far off. It will permit you to for all time broaden your wellbeing bar.

Essence #2

Reach where Cal can slide down the rope, and two additional ropes are visible somewhere far off. Your task is to reach the lower edge with the essence set apart in the screenshot 1. You need to relinquish the rope during the descent and take hold of the climbing wall underneath the secret. Essence guarantees XP.

Treasures #3-#5

Every one of the 3 datadisks are in the same area. Reach the area in the above images. Here you need to take hold of a rope and ride through successive rings.

During the ride, you must give up and hop down onto a passing stage. Track down every one of the 3 treasures at this area.

Assembly Staging

List of secrets of the Assembly Staging region

There are **11 collectibles** to find here:

- Chests: 2

- Essences: 1

- Databanks: 3

- Treasures: 5

Databank #1 - Ghosts in the Machine

Force Echo can be found shortly after arriving in the Assembly Staging from the Automated Forge side.

Treasure #1

Move to a higher edge in the same place where the first collectible was. In the spot from the image you will track down a Datadisc.

Chest #1

Stay in the first location and explore the area to the left of the green gate. The chest contains a track which can be played at the cantina on Koboh.

Treasure #2

Reach the pit with the monsters from picture 1. Bounce inside, manage the creatures and track down a Datadisc by one of the walls.

Essence #1

Start from the spot you view as the previous collectible. Cal can snatch drones that move upward. Use it to reach a higher edge with Essence, which increases the Power bar.

Databank #2 - Lifter Droid

After getting the previous 2 collectibles, climb to the area with an inactive droid to scan.

Treasure #3

The Datadisc is on the floor in the same location where the previous collectible was.

Treasure #4

The Datadisc is where you keep away from electric discharge and bounce over a slope to ledges. You will find the secret when you reach a bigger stable edge.

Treasure #5

In the wake of gathering the previous collectible, keep investigating the region with discharges. In the wake of playing out a wall run, assault the Scavenger droid rapidly - use an assault or toss a lightsaber. It will drop a Datadisc.

Databank #3 - Destroyed Wall

You can also scan a part of a structure in the same place where the Scavenger Droid was, You can do it before grabbing the zipline.

Chest #2 - Stim Canister

This is a risky collectible because you need to reach the side region of the Assembly Staging from the image. You can gain from one of the NPCs about the possibility of investigating it and opening a discretionary Gossip (not expected to get the secret).

You must start in the fundamental piece of the area and use the climbing walls and running walls from Picture 1. You will reach the zipline. Land on the edge from picture 2, however solely after Cal is close to it (a tumble from level could kill him).

In a huge heater like area, reach another zipline and keep away from electric discharges while using it (picture 1). You will reach an edge with a yellow chest concealing a Stim Canister, which will increase the times BD-1 can mend you by 1 forever.

Superstructure Fabricators

List of Superstructure Fabricators secrets

There are **2 collectibles** to find here:

- Databanks: 2

Databank #1 - Broken Droid

Reach the place where Cal can grab the ropes. Use them to reach the shelf marked in picture 1, where there is a droid to scan.

Databank #2 - Dagan's Long Shot

The secret is in the room where you fought Drya Thornne and unlocked the Crossguard stance. After the boss battle is over, you can find a meditation point - examine the echoand watch the recording.

Array Channel

List of secrets of the Array Channel region

There are **8 collectibles** to find here:

- Chests: 1
- Essences: 1
- Databanks: 5
- Treasures: 1

Databank #1 - Wavelength Honing Controls

The secret can be found just after using the Lift on the large blockade and entering the Array Channel. You have to scan the terminal

Databank #2 - One Stop Shop

You will find the Power Reverberation on the left side in the wake of going through the first passage, where you keep away from the stream of energy of the mining gun.

Chest #1

You can reach the chest where you push your opponents against the energy stream of the digging cannon interestingly.

Subsequent to disposing of the multitude of enemies, use the zipline at the spot from Picture 1 to run on the walls.

Cal will ultimately reach a higher edge, where, notwithstanding the droid, is also a chest with a thing of dress.

Databank #3 - Waking Giants

After acquiring the previous collectible, return to the lower level, bypass the large stream of energy, and reach the control room from where you can see the mining cannon.

Treasure #1

Soon in the wake of gathering the previous secret slide down the upward wall, move to one side on the climbing walls, and stay away from discharges. The collectible is at the feet of the second climbing wall. Leap to it, slide down, and catch Datadisc before Cal falls into the abyss.

Databank #4 - Ionizing Calibrators

Just after collecting the previous secret, climb to the new larger ledge and scan the post.

Databank #5 - Prized Merchandise

Subsequent to passing an extensive section of wall running, you will reach a long passage where you need to keep away from the stream of energy of the mining gun by passing through green gates and concealing in the side spaces. The Power Reverberation is in the first one - analyze it subsequent to destroying the droids.

Essence #1

In the same section where the previous collectible was, reach the last room on the right. There you will find an Essence that allocates XP.

Republic Research Laboratory

Republic Research Laboratory

There are **10 collectibles** to find here:

- Chests: 3
- Essences: 1
- Databanks: 5
- Treasures: 1

Databank #1 - Laboratory Thermoregulator

Scan the post next to the meditation point.

Databank #2 - The Plan

The reverberation is in the corridor with a glass wall through which you can see the reflection point. From the save point, you need to go through an area monitored by droids and Commotion Raiders.

Chest #1

In the same region, there is a world class Uproar Thief to overcome. When he is dead, search for the congested green passage from picture 1.

At the lower level, you must solve the mandatory riddle with a circle enhancer in the Republic Research Lab - we described it in the Puzzles page.

Subsequent to actuating the sphere enhancer, use the Koboh Processor on the energy shaft to guide it to the floor (picture 1). The dark vines will be set ablaze - you can now go through the green boundary. In the area in picture 2 you must furthermore use Power Lift to open the entryway. You will find a terminal that will open the choice to hack Droidekas (droids with a defensive shield around them).

Databank #3 - Disaster Strikes

This echo is near the orb amplifier associated with the previous collectible. This is the room where you catch the orb and place it in the amplifier.

Databank #4 - Inoperable Console

Scan the terminal in the small circular area of the lab, where Cal will unlock an upgraded Ascension Cable for grabbing onto balloons.

Chest #2

The chest is in the focal corridor and you can sling yourself to it from the inflatable subsequent to opening the overhauled Ascension Link. When plundered, it contains an appearance thing for Cal.

Databank #5 - Stabilizer Beam

While bouncing off of the balloons in the central room, reach the shelf with a purple energy beam and scan it.

Essence #1

The essence will show up in the room where you had the boss battle with Rayvis - you must loss him first. You will acquire an advantage that extends the block bar.

Chest #3

The locked chest is on one of the shelves in the focal corridor - you will reach it in the wake of catapulting from the inflatable.

You must have the BD-1 Electro Dart opened by gaining sufficient headway in the story. Use the dart on the distant blue fuse shown in the image, then rapidly plunder the briefly opened compartment. In the chest you will track down a cosmetic thing.

Treasure #1

The datadisc is on one of the round shelves in the central room. Launch yourself of the balloons and run on a few walls.

Nova Garon

Hanga Bay Exterior

List of secrets of the Hangar Bay Exterior region

There are 3 collectiblesto find here:

- Chests: 1
- Databanks: 1
- Treasures: 1

Databank #1 - IBB Database

You have to scan the wall in the hangar where the Mantis is.

Treasure #1

A Priorite Shard is in one of the side corridors adjacent to the hangar.

Chest #1

Star Wars Jedi: Survivor: The Complete Official Guide & Walkthrough

After picking up the previous collectible, turn 180 degrees and climb the vertical wall. At the end of the highest ledge is the BD-1 materials chest.

Hangar Bay

List of secrets of the Hangar Bay region

There are 6 collectibles to find here:

- Chests: 1

- Essences: 1

- Databanks: 3

- Treasures: 1

Databank #1 - Electron Wall

You will find the area to scan after descending the vertical wall from the side of the Hangar Bay Exterior location.

Treasure #1

You will track down a Priorite Shard in the corridor behind the area to scan connected with the previous collectible.

Databank #2 - Mind Trick Sabotage

A ForceEcho is at the terminal in the following room after the one with the ISB specialist. You will get to the area with the collectible by requesting BD-1 to hack, and you must go this way in the primary storyline.

Chest #1

The chest is in a larger room and you get to it by bouncing off the balloon. The container conceals a clothing item.

Databank #3 - Back-up Servers

The server to be scanned is in the room where the group of opponents was.

Essence #1

You can find the essence shortly in the wake of getting the previous collectible. Leave the server room and head in the opposite bearing to the mission objective marker. Cal's Power bar will be broadened.

Central Command

List of secrets to be found at Central Command

There are 7 collectibles to find here:

- Chest: 2

- Databanks: 2

- Treasures: 3

Databank #1 - Checkpoint

The place to be scanned is in a side room adjacent to the central room, where you defeated waves of enemies.

Treasure #2

The priorite shard is in a side room adjacent to the central room, where you defeat waves of enemies.

Treasure #1

The Priorite Shard is in the area adjacent to the octagonal platform with droids.

Chest #1

You must sling out of the inflatable and reach the ledges over the octagonal stage. In the chest you will track down weapon materials.

Databank #2 - Officer's uniform

After meeting Denvik (a cutscene) and putting on the officer's disguise, stay in the command center and scan the locker from the screenshot.

Chest #2 - Map Upgrade: Databank

Stay in the command room where you found the previous secret. BD-1 can hack the terminal shown in the screenshot. From now on, the holographic map will mark all databank secrets, i.e. echoes and objects to be scanned.

Treasure #3

Reach the spot shown in the screenshot. Cal can squeeze between the pipes.

In the new area, use the climbing wall from screenshot 1. At the point when you reach the top, turn towards the edge with the priorite shard - it is shown in screenshot 2. You should simply take a twofold leap.

Officer's quarters

List of secrets to be found at Officers' quarters

There are 3 collectibles to find here:

- Essence: 1
- Databanks: 2

Databank #1 - Voice message

You must reach Bode's quarters while using the officer's disguise. Examine the tent from the corner of the room.

Databank #2 - Family Portrait

Stay in the quarters and scan the painting on one of the walls showing Bode's family.

Essence #1

You can get this secret during the following visit to Nova Garon, because whilst being disguised as an officer in the primary storyline, the game won't permit you to open the entryway.

Reach the side entryway in the quarters, which is close to Bode's quarters. At the point when you open them, you will track down an essence that grants you XP.

Tanalorr

Planet Tanalorr

List of secrets to be found on Tanalorr

There are a total of 7 secrets across all Tanalorr regions:

- Databanks: 7

Databank #1 - Droids of the High Republic

Region: Haven's Edge

You will find the smashed droid by the rocks next to the Mantis, at which you begin exploring the planet.

Databank #2 - Jedi meditation site

Region: Haven's Edge

The place to be scanned is also located near Mantis's landing location.

Databank #3 - Buried invasion

Region: Verdant Gardens

You have to scan the wreck in the first part of the gardens.

Databank #4 - The Last Stand

Region: Verdant Gardens

After squeezing between the rocks, investigate the echo next to a shallow body of water.

Databank #5 - Ceremonial Fountain

Region: Verdant Gardens

You must scan the fountain just before entering the next region.

Databank #6 - Last call

Region: Audience Chamber

You can gather this and the following secret in the wake of overcoming the last boss, because you want to investigate the region where you dueled him. You will track down the reverberation at the entry to the destroyed field.

Database #7 - The Jedi Order credo

Region: Audience Chamber

The echo is by a damaged section of wall on the lower level of the arena.

ABOUT THE AUTHOR

Much thanks to you for perusing this Star Wars Jedi: Survivor guide! I have endeavored to welcome you the most extensive guide on Star Wars Jedi: Survivor that exists, and that implies the guide will be written in a special manner.

Made in United States
North Haven, CT
14 June 2024